SCENES AND MONOLOGUES OF SPIRITUAL EXPERIENCE

from the BEST CONTEMPORARY PLAYS

SCENES AND MONOLOGUES OF SPIRITUAL EXPERIENCE

from the BEST CONTEMPORARY PLAYS

Edited by

ROGER ELLIS

APPLAUSE
THEATRE & CINEMA BOOKS

An Imprint of Hal Leonard Corporation

Published in 2013 by Applause Theatre & Cinema Books
An Imprint of Hal Leonard Corporation
7777 West Bluemound Road
Milwaukee, WI 53213

Trade Book Division Editorial Offices
33 Plymouth St., Montclair, NJ 07042

Play Sources and Acknowledgments can be found on pages 291–295, which constitute an extension of this copyright page.

Printed in the United States of America

Book design by UB Communications

Library of Congress Cataloging-in-Publication Data is available upon request.

ISBN 978-1-4803-3156-3

www.applausebooks.com

CONTENTS

Introduction by Roger Ellis   xi

SCENES FOR A MAN
AND A WOMAN

*CREATION OF THE WORLD   3
by Arthur Miller

AVOW   11
by Bill C. Davis

*CHAGRIN FALLS   17
by Mia McCullough

DOG SEES GOD: CONFESSIONS OF   22
A TEENAGE BLOCKHEAD
by Bert V. Royal

MINOR LEAGUES   25
by Gustavo Ott

ANGELS IN AMERICA PART ONE: 31
MILLENNIUM APPROACHES
by Tony Kushner

CONVIVENCIA   36
by R. N. Sandberg

PILGRIMS MUSA AND SHERI   40
IN THE NEW WORLD
by Yussef El Guindi

IN THE SHAPE OF A WOMAN   51
by Tammy Ryan

SOME PEOPLE HAVE ALL THE LUCK   55
by Cándido Tirado

GOLDEN CHILD   62
by David Henry Hwang

LYNETTE AT 3 A.M.   66
by Jane Anderson

FROM EVERY MOUNTAINSIDE   71
by Max Bush

SCENES FOR TWO WOMEN

*AGNES OF GOD   85
by John Pielmeier

REINCARNATION   91
by Jessica Litwak

MARISOL   112
by José Rivera

DOUBT: A PARABLE   119
by John Patrick Shanley

FAT CHICKS   127
by Gustavo Ott

IN THE NEXT ROOM OR THE
VIBRATOR PLAY   133
by Sarah Ruhl

THROWN BY ANGELS   136
by Gwendolyn Schwinke

CELL CYCLE   142
by Cristina Pippa

CELL CYCLE   147
by Cristina Pippa

GIDION'S KNOT — 152
by Johnna Adams

SCENES FOR TWO MEN

GRACE — 175
by Mick Gordon and A. C. Grayling

MASS APPEAL — 180
by Bill. C. Davis

NEXT FALL — 191
by Geoffrey Nauffts

TURTLE ISLAND BLUES — 197
by William Borden

DOG SEES GOD: CONFESSIONS OF A TEENAGE BLOCKHEAD — 200
by Bert V. Royal

TIES THAT BIND: FEATURING THE ASTOUNDING KRISPINSKY — 204
by Eric Coble

FAMILY DEVOTIONS — 209
by David Henry Hwang

OUR LADY OF 121ST STREET — 214
by Stephen Adly Guirgis

OUR LADY OF 121ST STREET — 220
by Stephen Adly Guirgis

MONOLOGUES FOR WOMEN

*BEIRUT ROCKS — 227
by Israel Horovitz

MARISOL — 229
by José Rivera

THE LARK 231
by Jean Anouilh; translated by Christopher Fry

THIS BEAUTIFUL CITY 234
by Steven Cosson and Jim Lewis

THIS BEAUTIFUL CITY 236
by Steven Cosson and Jim Lewis

ME AND JOAN (OF ARC) 238
by Karen Sunde

THE ARAB-ISRAELI COOKBOOK 240
by Robin Soans

THE ARAB-ISRAELI COOKBOOK 242
by Robin Soans

*GIDION'S KNOT 245
by Johnna Adams

MONOLOGUES FOR MEN

*WAKE ME WHEN IT'S OVER 251
by Sybil St. Claire

BENGAL TIGER AT 253
THE BAGHDAD ZOO
by Rajiv Joseph

THE CONTROVERSY OF 257
VALLADOLID
by Jean-Claude Carrière

THE CONTROVERSY OF 260
VALLADOLID
by Jean-Claude Carrière

*PILGRIMS MUSA AND SHERI 263
IN THE NEW WORLD
by Yussef El Guindi

GOLDEN CHILD   265
by David Henry Hwang

*IN THE SHAPE OF A WOMAN   267
by Tammy Ryan

THIS BEAUTIFUL CITY   269
by Steven Cosson and Jim Lewis

IN A KINGDOM BY THE SEA   271
by Karen Sunde

*A TUESDAY IN APRIL   273
by Max Bush

*SPEAKING WELL OF THE DEAD   278
by Israel Horovitz

Working Up the Scene or Monologue   281

Play Sources and Acknowledgments   291

NOTES ON PRESENTING MONOLOGUES AND SCENES

An asterisk (*) beside the title indicates the editor's opinion of which scenes and monologues can permit gender-neutral casting.

INTRODUCTION

This book contains more than fifty monologues and two-character scenes from contemporary plays. It serves actors, directors, acting students, and their teachers as a resource for auditions and acting classes. The anthology contains both comic and serious material, drawing on outstanding theatrical writing from North America and Europe. Some of the plays from which the extracts are drawn are published properties, while others are very new and still unpublished. The final pages of the anthology contain suggestions for interpreting and staging these materials, for actors in need of a structured approach to performing in auditions or in studio scenes.

My primary concern in selecting the extracts for the book has been to identify the best theatrical writing for the stage. In order to accomplish this, I've restricted myself to extracts from plays that have been professionally produced within the past thirty years. With few exceptions, I've been able to do this, thus ensuring that the material has not simply been tested and developed for live audiences in the playhouse, but also is relevant, fresh and original. I've also used my own judgment in assessing the stage-worthiness of many of the extracts I've included. I've frequently used many of these monologues and scenes in my acting classes and workshops.

In building the collection, I've also tried to focus only on scenes and monologues with young characters (sixteen to thirty-five years old), thus privileging younger actors who are constantly seeking new audition material. The exceptions to this rule occur in certain plays, such as Gustavo Ott's *Minor Leagues*, Tammy Ryan's *In the Shape of a Woman*, or Bill C. Davis's *Mass Appeal*, where only one of the actors or actresses is very young. And readers should also note the table of contents, where I've indicated those selections where some gender-neutral casting is possible; that is, not all dramatic material must always be presented according to the gender-based role breakdown found in the original script. In fact, a large number of scenes, and especially the monologues in this anthology, can be effectively performed by either a male or female actor in the role.

Finally, readers will also note differences between all the monologues in terms of length: some are as short as sixty seconds, while others may run on to several minutes. Certainly, the sixty-second monologues may seem ready-made for auditions, which often require no more than two minutes of prepared material (i.e., a pair of contrasting monologues). Bear in mind, though, that longer speeches may be edited down in order to conform to audition requirements.

Longer monologues are also useful to include in this sort of class resource because they challenge actors to learn how to sustain concentration and development in longer pieces. Many acting classes and workshops, for example, are devoted to this sort of training, particularly nowadays when so many one-person shows have become popular. But a longer monologue can also serve the actor as excellent material for strengthening his or her sight-reading skills. One of the most valuable training exercises an actor can perform is to pursue a daily program of sight-reading "off the page" with unfamiliar material. This skill is absolutely necessary for presenting good cold readings, and longer dramatic monologues are excellent tools to work with.

Whether the monologues seem long or short, however, is not important. What's important is for the actor to play the heartbeats in the piece, regardless of the number of lines.

SPIRITUALITY AND THE COLLECTION

As the title of the book indicates, this anthology is governed by the theme of "spiritual experience." I use this term broadly to include not only spiritual issues that directly affect established religions, but also those issues that have been traditionally viewed through the lens of organized religion but that now, in our secular age, force individuals to grapple with problems without the support of religious teaching. For example, churchmen of every sect have long busied themselves with problems of clerical celibacy, conflicting belief systems, or killing others in a "just war." On the other hand, many today prefer to regard issues such as substance abuse, suicide, capital punishment, or abortion simply as matters of social justice and human rights. Thus, our modern age is no longer bound by sectarian interpretations of God and the supernatural; instead, we confront a spiritual landscape populated by voices proclaiming the values of Judaism, Christianity, reincarnation, Buddhism, zombies, jihad, astrology, ghostbusting, tribal beliefs, and many other "spiritual perspectives" that are widely reflected in the playhouse.

I've tried to represent as many of these perspectives as possible in this limited collection while still remaining faithful to the major artistic criteria mentioned above; I believe readers will be pleasantly surprised by the wide range of philosophical and theatrical excitement they encounter in a body of plays dealing with "spiritual experience." *Angels in America*, for example, certainly expresses a rather novel interpretation of how "angels" busy themselves in contemporary American society; the same might be said of José

Rivera's *Marisol*, where the angel character seems more like a military recruiting officer preparing for Armageddon than a traditional ambassador of heaven. Yet, both plays pose disturbing philosophical questions as well as exciting theatrical challenges to audiences and theater practitioners alike.

This is not to say that contemporary playwrights are pushing organized religion to the back burner by focusing attention on humanitarian solutions to social problems, or by debunking Christianity, Mormonism, and other faiths. On the contrary, there are numerous examples of contemporary inspirational or devotional religious plays attracting large audiences to our playhouses. Think, for example, of the many productions and Broadway successes that plays such as *Godspell, Doubt, Agnes of God*, or *Mass Appeal* have achieved over the years. In fact, there are several monologues and scenes in this collection dealing with Joan of Arc, whose life has inspired modern audiences for generations.

It is noteworthy that before now, no anthology has gathered this kind of dramatic material into a single collection. It may surprise some readers to consider that so many contemporary plays deal with aspects of religious faith. The fact remains, however, that a concern for religion and the supernatural—and a focus on moral and spiritual problems—has permeated Western dramatic writing for at least the past century. Plays inspired in whole or in part by the life of the spirit continue to fascinate playwrights and challenge our most talented theater artists even today.

A FINAL REMINDER

Many of the scenes in this collection can be presented as stand-alone pieces on an entertainment program. In fact, one of them, Jessica Litwak's *Reincarnation*, is a one-act play in its own right. If you wish to present any of these selections as part of a public program, live or electronic, you must always request permission from the playwright or his or her agent before you do so.

Perhaps this caution needs to be restated in this Internet age, where so much is available to us online or otherwise reproducible at little or no charge. Readers must remind themselves that plays—like other unique cultural artifacts—are not equivalent to the bytes and factoids we slog through and digitally manipulate by the thousands every day. They are the intellectual property of human beings who have spent many years earning, and who therefore deserve, proper acknowledgement and compensation for producing and distributing their work to the public.

Bear in mind that I'm attempting in this book to highlight and promote the work of a handful of uniquely talented and highly motivated artists whose worth, importance, and cultural value in our world is already deeply discounted, frequently ridiculed, and in some cases even despised. Their plays are their honest work, their "products." Pay for them. I've provided relevant contact information in the acknowledgements.

Roger Ellis

SCENES FOR A MAN
AND A WOMAN

CREATION OF THE WORLD
BY ARTHUR MILLER

Unlike the traditionally serious Biblical account of Adam and Eve, this version suggests that the creation of humans was more improvisational and arbitrary. Here, GOD becomes a petulant scientific experimenter, while LUCIFER tries to straighten HIM out with common sense. This comic dialogue can be staged very simply on a bare stage with a minimum of physical props and furniture. The male-female roles are easily interchangeable because the characters' genders are non-specific. The scene becomes most effective when actors play it directly to the audience, as though the spectators themselves were also overlooking the Garden of Eden. The roles in this scene can be played by either gender.

(*Alone,* GOD *looks down at the earth, as* LUCIFER *enters.*)

GOD: All right, go ahead, say it.

LUCIFER: Nothing for me to say, Lord. (HE *points below.*) You see it as well as I.

GOD: (*Looking down, shaking* HIS *head.*) What did I do wrong?

LUCIFER: Why look at it that way? They're beautiful, they help each other, they praise You every few minutes—

GOD: Lucifer, they don't multiply.

LUCIFER: Maybe give them a few more years . . .

GOD: But there's no sign of anything. Look at them—the middle of a perfect, moonlit night, and they're playing handball.

LUCIFER: Well, You wanted them innocent.

GOD: Every once in a while, though, he does seem to get aroused.

LUCIFER: Aroused, yes, but what's the good if he doesn't get it in the right place? And when he does, she walks off to pick a flower or something.

GOD: I can't figure that out. (*Pause.* THEY *stare down.*)

LUCIFER: Of course, You could always— (HE *breaks off.*)

GOD: What?

LUCIFER: Look, I don't want to mix in, and then You'll say I'm criticizing everything—

GOD: I don't know why I stand for your superciliousness.

LUCIFER: At least I don't bore You like the rest of these spirits.

GOD: Sometimes I'd just as soon you did. What have you got in mind?

LUCIFER: Now, remember, You asked me.

GOD: What have you got in mind!

LUCIFER: You see? You're mad already.

GOD: (*Roaring furiously.*) I am not mad!

LUCIFER: All right, all right. You could take her back and restring her insides. Reroute everything, so wherever he goes in it connects to the egg.

GOD: No—no—no, I don't want to fool with that. She's perfect now; I'm not tearing her apart again. Out of the question.

LUCIFER: Well, then. You've only got one other choice. You've got to thin out the innocence down there. (GOD *turns to him suspiciously.*) See? You're giving me that look again; whatever I say, You turn it into some kind of plot. Like when You made that fish with the fur on. Throw him in the ocean, and all the angels run around singing hosannas. I come in and tell You the thing's drowned, and You're insulted.

GOD: Yes. But I—I've stopped making fish with fur any more.

LUCIFER: But before I can penetrate with a fact, I've got to go through hell.

GOD: (HE *suddenly points down.*) He's putting his arm around her. (LUCIFER *looks down.*) Lucifer! (THEY *both stretch over the edge to see better.*) Lucifer! (*Suddenly* HIS *expression changes to incredulity, then anger, and* HE *throws up* HIS *hands in futile protest.*) Where in the world does he get those stupid ideas!

LUCIFER: (*Still looking down.*) Now he's going to sleep.

GOD: Oh, dear, dear, dear, dear. (HE *sits disconsolately.*)

LUCIFER: Lord, the problem down there is that You've made it all so perfect. Everything they look at is not only good, it's especially good. The sun is good, rats are good, fleas are good, the moon, lions, athlete's foot—every single thing is just as good as every other thing. Because, naturally, You created everything, so everything's as attractive as everything else.

GOD: What's so terrible about perfection? Except that you can't stand it.

LUCIFER: Well, simply—if You want him to go into her, into the right place, and stay there long enough, You'll have to make that part better.

GOD: I am not remaking that woman.

LUCIFER: It's not necessary. All I'm saying is that sex has to be made not just good, but—well, terrific. Right now he'd just as soon pick his nose. In other words, You've got to rivet his attention on that one place.

GOD: How would I do that?

LUCIFER: Well, let's look at it. What is the one thing that makes him stop whatever he's doing and pay strict attention?

GOD: What?

LUCIFER: You, Lord. Soon as You appear, he, so to speak, comes erect. Give sex that same sort of holiness in his mind, the same sort of hope that is never discouraged and never really fulfilled, the same fear of being unacceptable. Make him feel toward sex as he feels toward You, and You're in—*unbeschreiblich*! Between such high promise and deadly terror, he won't be able to think of anything else. (*Pause.*)

GOD: How?

LUCIFER: Well . . . (HE *hesitates a long moment, until* GOD *slowly turns to* HIM *with a suspicious look.*) All right, look—there's no way around it, I simply have to talk about those apples.

GOD: (*Stamps* HIS *foot and stands, strides up and down, trying to control* HIS *temper.*) Lucifer!

LUCIFER: I refuse to believe that man's only way to demonstrate his love for God is to refuse to eat some fruit! That sort of game is simply unworthy of my father!

GOD: (*Angered.*) Really now!

LUCIFER: Forgive me, sir, but I am useless to You if I don't speak my mind. May I tell you why I think You planted that tree in the garden? (**GOD** *is silent, but consenting, even if unwillingly.*) Objectively speaking, it is senseless. You wanted Adam's praise for everything You made, absolutely innocent of any doubt about Your goodness. Why, then, plant a fruit which can only make him wise, sophisticated, and analytical? May I continue? (**GOD** *half-willingly nods.*) He certainly will begin to question everything if he eats an apple, but why is that necessarily bad? (**GOD** *looks surprised, angering.*) He'll not only marvel that the flower blooms, he will ask why and discover chlorophyll—and bless You for chlorophyll. He'll not only praise You that food makes him strong, he will discover his bile duct and praise You for his pancreas. He may lose his innocence, but the more he learns of Your secrets, the more reasons he will have to praise You. And that is why, quite without consciously knowing it, You planted that tree there. It was Your fantastic inner urge to magnify Your glory to the last degree. In six words, Lord, You wanted full credit for everything.

GOD: He must never eat those apples.

LUCIFER: Then why have You tempted him? What is the point?

GOD: I wanted him to wake each morning, look at that tree, and say, "For God's sake I won't eat these apples." Not even one.

LUCIFER: Fine. But with that same absence of curiosity he is not investigating Eve.

GOD: But the other animals manage.

LUCIFER: Their females go into heat, and the balloon goes up. But Eve is ready almost any time, and that means no time. It's part of that whole dreadful uniformity down there.

GOD: They are my children; I don't want them to know evil.

LUCIFER: Why call it evil? One apple, and he'll know the difference between good and better. And once he knows that, he'll be all over her. (**HE** *looks down.*) Look, he's kissing a tree. You see? The damned fool has no means of discriminating.

GOD: (*Looking down.*) Well, he should kiss trees too.

LUCIFER: Fine. If that's the way You feel, You've got Adam and Eve, and it'll be a thousand years before You're a grandfather. (**HE** *stands.*) Think it over. I'd be glad to go down and—(**GOD** *gives him a look.*) I'm only trying to help!

GOD: Lucifer, I'm way ahead of you.

LUCIFER: Lord, that's inevitable.

GOD: Stay away from that tree.

LUCIFER: (*With a certain evasiveness.*) Whatever You say, sir. May I go now?

GOD: (*After a pause.*) Don't have the illusion that I am in conflict about this; I mean, don't decide to go down there and do Me a favor, or something. I know perfectly well why I put that tree there.

LUCIFER: (*Surprised.*) Really!

GOD: Yes, really. I am in perfect control over my subconscious, friend. It was not to tempt Adam; it's I who was tempted. I finished him and I saw he was beautiful, and for a moment I loved him beyond anything I had ever made—and I thought, maybe I should let him see through the rose petal to its chemistry, the formation of amino acids to the secrets of life. His simple praise for surfaces made me impatient to show him the physics of My art, which would raise him to a God.

LUCIFER: Why'd You change Your mind?

GOD: Because I thought of what became of you. The one angel who really understands biology and physics, the one I loved before all the rest and took such care to teach—and you can't take a breath without thinking how to overthrow Me and take over the universe!

LUCIFER: Lord, I only wanted them to know more, the more to praise You!

GOD: The more they know, the less they will need Me, Lucifer; you know that as well as I! And that's all you're after, to grind away their respect for Me. "Give them an apple!" If it weren't for the Law of the Conservation of Energy I would destroy you! Don't go near that tree or those dear people—not in any form, you hear? They are innocent, and innocent they will remain till I turn the lights out forever! (GOD *goes out,* LUCIFER *is alone.*)

LUCIFER: Now what is He *really* saying? He put it there to tempt *Himself*! Therefore He's not of one mind about innocence; and how could He be when innocence blinds Adam to half the wonders He has made? I will help the Lord. Yes, that's the only way to put it; I'm His helper. I open up the marvels He dares not show, and thereby magnify His glory. In short, I disobey what He says and carry out what He means, and if that's evil, it's only to do good. Strange—I never felt so close to my creator as I do right now! Once Adam eats, he'll multiply, and Lucifer completes the lovely world of God! Oh, praise the Lord who gave me all this insight! My fight with Him is over! Now evil be my good, and Eve and Adam multiply in blessed sin! Make way, dumb stars, the world of man begins!

AVOW
BY BILL C. DAVIS

The issue of celibacy in the Catholic Church has been hotly debated in recent years. In the following scene, FATHER RAYMOND meets IRENE for the first time. HE has denied HER brother a request to be married in the church, and SHE has come to question FATHER RAYMOND about that decision. As the play develops, FATHER RAYMOND and IRENE grow more attracted to each other, until the question of HIS leaving the priesthood in order to pursue HIS love for HER becomes a major issue in HIS—and HER—life. The following scene introduces this growing relationship, only hesitantly touching upon the chemistry that begins to emerge between the two characters.

IRENE: Hello, Father. Thank you for seeing me.

FATHER RAYMOND: You're Brian's sister?

IRENE: Right. Irene.

FATHER RAYMOND: You play the piano.

IRENE: Yes.

FATHER RAYMOND: And you make a living at it.

IRENE: I do. A minor miracle. I get booked around the country to play with different orchestras. I have an agent. You know—the whole thing.

FATHER RAYMOND: That's wonderful. It really must be like a vocation.

IRENE: Exactly. That's what it is—a vocation. Sometimes when I'm interviewed they ask, "When did you decide to be a pianist?" I can't answer that. It's like asking my brother, "When did you decide to be gay?"

FATHER RAYMOND: Well—no—actually, that would be different. Being a pianist is a vocation. Being gay is . . .

IRENE: A fact. A simple fact.

FATHER RAYMOND: Simple for who? (*Pause.*) Would you like some coffee?

IRENE: No. I'm off coffee for a while—but thanks. I wanted to meet you because Brian and Tom speak so highly of you.

FATHER RAYMOND: Still?

IRENE: Yes, you see, for some reason, the Church really matters to my brother, and to Tom.

FATHER RAYMOND: (*Ironically.*) Amazing, isn't it?

IRENE: It is. And I can't understand why you want to blow it. I mean, isn't your membership waning—big time?

FATHER RAYMOND: The Church isn't a department store. And we're not trying to win customers.

IRENE: I understand that. But still I was hoping that I could help you look at their situation a little differently.

FATHER RAYMOND: I'm open to be helped.

IRENE: I wanted to . . . suggest that maybe Brian and Tom's love is a mystery to be honored as much as any other mystery in the

Church. And in light of that why couldn't you announce their desire to be married from the pulpit the way you do with any other couple that falls in love?

FATHER RAYMOND: You're living in a dream world.

IRENE: This from a man who changes bread and wine into the body and blood of Christ every Sunday?

FATHER RAYMOND: Not only every Sunday—every *day*.

IRENE: You've got human bone fragments in your altars; you burn incense; you have consecrated ground and exorcisms. *I'm* in a dream world? The *Church* is in a dream world and the problem is that you guys won't let anybody else's dream wake you up.

FATHER RAYMOND: The problem is that every spoiled brat who has a whim wants it sanctioned by the institutions that have been created to keep some semblance of moral order.

IRENE: My brother is not a spoiled brat!

FATHER RAYMOND: I didn't mean Brian specifically . . .

IRENE: Brian is the best Catholic I've ever known. He's the one who talked me into going through with this pregnancy.

FATHER RAYMOND: You're pregnant right now?

IRENE: Thank you for not noticing, but yes. I'm due in five months.

FATHER RAYMOND: Your husband didn't want a child?

IRENE: I'm not married.

FATHER RAYMOND: Are you planning to marry the father?

IRENE: I'm booked to go on a ten-city tour two months after I give birth.

FATHER RAYMOND: And the father?

IRENE: He's not going on tour.

FATHER RAYMOND: So is this pregnancy the result of something casual?

IRENE: No. It was essential; momentous; it was a turning point, but it wasn't permanent.

FATHER RAYMOND: Why not?

IRENE: He's married. We took precautions, but, as Brian put it, there was a higher purpose operating at the time.

FATHER RAYMOND: Irene—if there were a higher purpose, should you have been having an affair with a married man?

IRENE: I guess "higher" is the wrong word to use with you; deeper— a deeper purpose. Right and wrong had to be put on hold.

FATHER RAYMOND: Yes—I've heard that sort of thing on the top-forty countdown. "Something that feels so good can't be wrong . . ." blah, blah, blah.

IRENE: Look—I'm not going to try to justify what I did. I'm not proud of it, I'm just . . . I'm here as an ambassador for my brother who I love more than anyone in the world.

FATHER RAYMOND: He's lucky to have that kind of love.

IRENE: He deserves it. And he deserves the love of the Church.

FATHER RAYMOND: He has it.

IRENE: Prove it! Announce their names from the pulpit.

FATHER RAYMOND: Giving people what they want is not a proof of love.

IRENE: That's what I would expect to hear from a priest. (*Pause.*) Why did you become a priest?

FATHER RAYMOND: We don't have enough time.

IRENE: I have to ask, because it seems that most priests don't have a choice. You look at them and you think, "what else could they have been?" I look at you and I don't get that feeling. I mean— I could see you with a woman.

FATHER RAYMOND: (*Pause.*) About this baby . . .

IRENE: Did I embarrass you?

FATHER RAYMOND: No. Were you trying to?

IRENE: Was I?

FATHER RAYMOND: Are you planning to raise this child alone?

IRENE: Brian and Tom are going to adopt him.

FATHER RAYMOND: (*Pause.*) Oh. Oooookay. Ummm—do you know if they're intending to raise your child as a Catholic?

IRENE: Would you marry them if they were?

FATHER RAYMOND: No.

IRENE: But would you baptize their baby?

FATHER RAYMOND: Yes.

IRENE: Even though the parents aren't married?

FATHER RAYMOND: The point is the baby. Does it worry you that your child may be subjected to ridicule as he gets into junior high and high school?

IRENE: You think kids will pick on him because of his parents? No. Did kids pick on you for being celibate?

FATHER RAYMOND: What makes you think I was celibate when I was a teenager?

IRENE: Oh my God. You gave it up? You tasted of the fruit and you let it go?

FATHER RAYMOND: I have to go hear confessions now.

IRENE: I should hope so.

FATHER RAYMOND: *Hear* confessions.

IRENE: Do you have a confessor?

FATHER RAYMOND: I do. He's at another parish. (**HE** *shows* **HER** *to the door.*) Maybe someday you'll come to Mass at *this* parish with Brian and Tom.

IRENE: And maybe someday you'll tell me whether or not you're a virgin.

FATHER RAYMOND: It's immaterial. But I'm flattered you're interested.

IRENE: Well—we're making progress. I've been able to flatter you.

CHAGRIN FALLS
BY MIA McCULLOUGH

Everyone in Chagrin Falls, Oklahoma, is connected with killing, employed either in the town's slaughterhouse or in the penitentiary, or serving the visitors, families, and employees of both places. PATRICE is a graduate student who has come to do a story about an inmate scheduled to be executed. In the following scene, SHE interviews the prison chaplain about an upcoming execution. The REVEREND is struggling with the challenges to HIS Christian faith that confront HIM in Chagrin Falls: Can HE hate the sin but love the sinner? Is capital punishment really the will of God? THEIR conversation takes place outdoors and is very tense as both characters try to make small talk in order to offset the strain of the upcoming execution. The role of PATRICE in this scene can be played as a male or as a female.

REVEREND: It's pretty, isn't it? All that wheat.

PATRICE: It's beautiful . . . I can't believe I've never seen it, touched it, before.

REVEREND: Yeah, it's one of those unexpected pleasures in a place like this. You really get to capture the pastoral elegance of your food. Before they chop it down or kill it.

PATRICE: Or hang it on the wall.

REVEREND: Yes. (**THEY** *both look up at the cow.*)

PATRICE: Well, I'll try to make this quick and painless. Do you mind? (**SHE** *lifts up the tape recorder.*)

REVEREND: No.

PATRICE: I never have to worry about misquoting people this way. (*The* **REVEREND** *leans toward the recorder.*)

REVEREND: John—with-an-H—Maycomb; thirty-eight; born and raised in New Canaan, Connecticut; Divinity School at Harvard; did two interim years in northern Michigan and then came here three years ago.

PATRICE: Do this much?

REVEREND: Every execution. Well, most of them.

PATRICE: Do you miss New England?

REVEREND: The landscape, but not the people.

PATRICE: You said you've been here three years?

REVEREND: A little over.

PATRICE: And how do you like it?

REVEREND: The job or the place?

PATRICE: Both.

REVEREND: The job is . . . challenging. And gratifying, most days. The place is . . . diffr'nt. The people are great. Open. Honest. Where I grew up, it was all closed doors and secrets and things left unsaid. There are no secrets in Chagrin Falls . . . which is a blessing and a curse, I suppose, but it's a quality I value. But it's a sad place.

PATRICE: How so?

REVEREND: Well, you know, it's a poor, rural community. People here don't really get to reach their full potential. Half the town works at the prison, which doesn't exactly foster a sense of contentment and well-being. The other half kills cows for a living or sits home raising children and watching soap operas. Sometimes I think every last person in Chagrin Falls is suffering from clinical depression. Except Henry Harcourt, of course. Henry kind of floats above it all. The rest of the town is steeped in death and Henry floats above it. I think it sort of makes everyone hate Henry, but only because they wish they had it in them. I think he's immune to it, somehow.

PATRICE: To what?

REVEREND: The despair.

PATRICE: Is it contagious?

REVEREND: I think all sorrow is contagious to some degree.

PATRICE: Have you caught it?

REVEREND: I don't know. I think I find it more compelling than catching. I don't know what that says about me, exactly, being drawn to other people's sorrow.

PATRICE: Well, it certainly explains why you've chosen this line of work.

REVEREND: I suppose.

PATRICE: How many executions have you done?

REVEREND: This will be fifteen.

PATRICE: Does it get easier or harder? (*Beat.*)

REVEREND: It gets easier to do, and harder to live with it afterwards.

PATRICE: How do you feel about capital punishment?

REVEREND: The Warden has asked me not to discuss my feelings on that issue with any more reporters.

PATRICE: OK, a different question, then. Ummm, during the execution, what exactly do you do?

REVEREND: Well, I walk with him to the death chamber. Stand aside while they strap him down and get the needle in his arm. Talk to him, if he seems to find any comfort in that. And then they pull the curtains so the spectators can see. And I say a prayer. If he wants. After he says his last words. And then the Warden signals the executioner. And we all stand there. Watching . . .

PATRICE: Does he pick the prayer, or do you?

REVEREND: If they have a specific passage they want me to read, I'll read it. Usually, they let me pick it.

PATRICE: What about Jonas?

REVEREND: I believe he's looking for a passage. Not that he can read very well, mind you, but he's enlisted the assistance of one of the corrections officers.

PATRICE: Not Thaddeus.

REVEREND: (*Smiling.*) No. I can't say I've ever seen Thaddeus reading the Bible.

PATRICE: I would think Jonas would enlist you to find an appropriate prayer.

REVEREND: Yes, well, he . . . hasn't asked.

Patrice: What do you think of Jonas Caldwell? (*Long pause.*)

Reverend: I think he is a very sad human being.

Patrice: Do you think he's changed at all, since his conviction?

Reverend: Changed? Well, I didn't know him then, but he hasn't made any kind of grand turn-around or found God, if that's what you mean. I don't think being incarcerated has improved Jonas's personality.

Patrice: Thaddeus says he spits at you.

Reverend: Yes, he does. That's really the only recourse he has anymore. That and flinging his feces at people. (*Pause.*) I don't like Jonas Caldwell. I won't lie to you. I'll even go so far as to say I really dislike him. He's a loathsome individual, bubbling over with hate. But I do have pity for him. I mean, he had a terrible childhood, a monster for a father, no one to help him along the way. I don't think an ounce of love was ever put into that man. There's no reason to think we should get any out of him. Still, I expect this will be the most difficult execution for me so far.

Patrice: Why's that?

Reverend: Because some very small and dark part of me will be glad when he is dead.

DOG SEES GOD: CONFESSIONS OF A TEENAGE BLOCKHEAD
BY BERT V. ROYAL

CB *is a high school stoner trying to deal with the puzzling emotions aroused by the death of* HIS *dog, and* HIS *sister is currently playing the role of a Goth. The characters don't regard themselves as ridiculous because* THEY *actually believe* THEY'VE *discovered spiritual truth contemplating the dog's demise.* CB *and* HIS SISTER *are standing beside each other and staring at a wooden cross in their backyard. A long silence passes.* SHE *takes a box of cigarettes out of* HER *purse (that is shaped like a coffin) and offers one to* HIM.

CB: Mom will kill you if she sees you smoking.

CB's SISTER: (*Lighting the cigarette.*) Well, when she does, I hope you'll have the decency to bury me in an actual cemetery rather than the backyard. (*Another long silence passes.*) Do you think we should say a prayer or something?

CB: I guess.

CB's SISTER: Okay. You can say it.

CB: I don't want to.

CB's SISTER: Well, neither do I!

CB: I don't know what to say.

CB's Sister: Oh, stop being so melodramatic, Charles. No one's asking for a eulogy. Just a simple prayer. Ask the Earth to watch over him. Or something.

CB: He's dead. There's not a whole lot of that necessary.

CB's Sister: You're so morbid. What about his next life? I think we should pray to Hecate and ask her to make him a human. Someone we meet and become friends with.

CB: What???

CB's Sister: Hecate is the Goddess of death. She's also a Goddess of reincarnation. It's Wiccan.

CB: Oh, so you're Wiccan this week? Glad that's cleared up. I can't keep your personalities straight! Last week, you go with a friend to a Baptist church, come home and proceed to tell Mom, Dad, and me that we're going to hell because we watch TV. A mere NINE DAYS LATER, you're Elvira, Mistress of the Dark. We can't keep up with you! FIND. AN. IDENTITY.

CB's Sister: You're one to talk!

CB: What could you possibly mean by that? I'm always the same!

CB's Sister: (*Venomously.*) That's nothing to brag about. (*Beat.*) Just drop it, okay? You don't tell me how to live my life and I won't tell you how to live yours. (*Silence.*)

CB: I thought there'd be a bigger turnout. (**She** *gives* **Him** *a funny look.*) Well, he was popular. All our friends loved him. I just thought people would actually show up to pay their respects.

CB's Sister: You invited our friends?

CB: A few.

CB's Sister: You are so embarrassing!

CB: You're dressed like the bride of Frankenstein and I'm embarrassing?

CB's Sister: Shut up about my dress!

CB: (*Sotto voce to self.*) This is not the way he would've wanted his funeral.

CB's Sister: He was a DOG, Charles. They shit on the ground and lick themselves. Ceremony is probably not key here. He was just a fucking dog.

CB: Oh yeah? Well, he was MY fucking dog. So, fuck you.

CB's Sister: He was my fucking dog, too! So, fuck you! (*Beat.*)

CB: He never liked you.

CB's Sister: I suppose he told you this.

CB: He didn't have to. It was apparent. He barely tolerated you.

CB's Sister: I hate you.

CB: Big loss.

CB's Sister: You're a dickhead, CB.

CB: (*Exploding.*) JUST SAY YOUR FUCKING PRAYER! (*Long pause.*)

CB's Sister: He was your fucking dog. You fucking say it. (**She** *storms off.*)

MINOR LEAGUES
BY GUSTAVO OTT

How difficult and painful it is for some people to accept death and let go of family members and loved ones who have passed! Sometimes the desire to keep the dead ones around as though they were still alive reaches absurd proportions. GOOSY *is an elderly American hustler, visiting a capitol city in South America during the Christmas season.* HE'S *acting as an agent for Martin, a wealthy North American collector of baseball cards, who has sent* GOOSY *to purchase a rare card. To* HIS *chagrin* HE *has learned that the seller is a fourteen-year-old girl,* VANESSA, *who refuses to be pinned down on the price. Instead,* SHE *moves into* HIS *swanky hotel suite for a few days while* SHE *considers the deal, amusing herself by playing baseball question-and-answer jokes with* HIM, *and showing* HIM HER *"paintings" of big cities done in colorful dots. The scene is cleverly constructed with a series of minor conflicts that gradually lead to the powerful climax in the scene where* GOOSY *suffers a heart attack.*

GOOSY: (*Threatening, facing* VANESSA.) My last, and final offer is sixty thousand. (*Looks at* HER.) So, what do you think?

VANESSA: Fine with me.

GOOSY: (HE *offers* HER HIS *hand.*) Deal?

Vanessa: It depends.

Goosy: DEPENDS ON WHAT?

Vanessa: Ninth Inning. You're down by one. Two outs and the count is three and one. Do you steal second?

Goosy: Second base. . . .

Vanessa: Do you steal or don't you?

Goosy: Yeah, sure.

Vanessa: No. You don't. You jeopardize the whole game.

Goosy: So what?

Vanessa: It's the game. The most important thing is the game. If you were really a fanatic there would only be one answer.

Goosy: So fine. Who sent you?

Vanessa: Sent what?

Goosy: Who do you work for?

Vanessa: I don't work.

Goosy: Maybe for Fleer? Who's paying you?

Vanessa: Mr. Fleer?

Goosy: An agency. A stinking agency that does everything it can to ruin me. And they do a good job. Well, I mean every time they've wanted to. . . .

Vanessa: I don't know anything about them.

Goosy: Two years ago they almost drove me out of the business completely. What do they care if I starve? Well—if you don't work for Fleer, how do you know so much?

VANESSA: It's got nothing to do with knowing so much. It's the game. Thinking about the game and the book. Have you heard about the book?

GOOSY: The book?

VANESSA: It's a handbook, one you keep in your head. An imaginary one. But it tells what you can and can't do. Experience shows how things work and what doesn't. Stick to the book, play conservative, play with experience. You go against the book, you take the risk. (**SHE** *moves over by* **HIS** *briefcase on the table. Goes far stage right. Turns to face* **HIM**.) You're up by eleven runs. You have a man on third. No outs. Do you make the squeeze play or not?

GOOSY: Sure, why not?

VANESSA: No. No. You don't. And you know why? It's a lack of respect for the other team. You don't need that run. There's no reason to humiliate the other team with your strength. The important thing is knowing how to win. Knowing how to win well. Knowing how to be strong. Respect for the losing team, because everyone who loses has something in his favor.

GOOSY: Losers have nothing, Vanessa.

VANESSA: Honor.

GOOSY: The winner has that.

VANESSA: Victory makes him forget.

GOOSY: I've lost plenty of times and it doesn't feel like honor. I've been sad, sure, disgusted, usually furious. Mostly, I feel hate, most of the time, but honor, that's—that's never. I don't know what you're talking about.

VANESSA: You're a businessman. Because you're not a fan.

GOOSY: I'd rather be what I am than some eleven-year-old girl who thinks she's got everything on her side!

VANESSA: I'm fourteen! There's no way I can talk with someone who doesn't love my game.

GOOSY: And you, what do you know about anything? How do you know I don't love baseball? Because I don't play along with your idiotic questions? So what? What does a fifteen-year-old girl know about anything? (*Begins furiously jamming papers into the briefcase.*) When I was young I wanted to be a player. A pitcher. Southpaw. I'd be there to put out the fires, the star relief. I'd be one of the greats. That dream lasted only two years because the war came. Just the name still terrifies me. It was over quick, but it was a nightmare every second. I only thank God I got wounded and could get out of that jungle. I don't want to go back there . . . even the name, out of my head—I don't want those memories. (*Slams briefcase shut.*) But when I got back I started getting pains, here in my arm, strong, sharp pains. They operated so I could never throw again. So I did painting. Florals, like Van Gogh, but cooler. Calming dots like Seurat. . . . Now, I know more about painting than MOMA. But, those sketches . . . there was always that one like that looked like shit, it never failed. That one line! And you paint your bridges and streets and buildings with dots. . . . Fucking dots, damn it! No baseball for me, no art, no game, nothing except: business.

VANESSA: Business . . . .

GOOSY: Yes, because business means MONEY, little girl. That's right, miss know-it-all. *MONEY.* The same reason you're here. The same reason you're driving such a hard bargain, MONEY. Di-Ne-Ro. Cash, Vanessa. Buying power. The secret to everything.

Vanessa: God loves the poor.

Goosy: But he takes such good care of the rich.

Vanessa: I'm not listening to you!

Goosy: Now you don't want to listen? We shouldn't talk about the money, filthy, dirty money. . . . Sure, what's it to you. You're fourteen. You're just a snot-nosed brat. You don't have responsibilities. But everyone, I . . . everyone has to pay. The car, the ex, the house, the restaurant, the pizza, my pacemaker. Michael's box. . . . Every Goddamn thing.

Vanessa: Box? Why box?

Goosy: Do you know when I found out the value of money? That day, I was shaving. I was stuck in front of the mirror, and I could see it on my face that my savings account was completely gone. I had hit rock bottom. There were no deposits. Only withdrawals. I've never been so terrified in my life; not even during the war.

Vanessa: What's Michael's box?

Goosy: It's none of your business. Leave me alone. (**Vanessa** *stares at* **Him**.) Michael's box . . . it's a cold place. A coffin where I've kept him for seven years. He had a stroke. He died. Michael's been frozen at one hundred ninety-six degrees below zero for seven years. He should be twenty-eight now, he is, and first baseman for the California Angels, or maybe the Dodgers. (*Walking away.*) Keeping him there is like a hope . . . maybe in the future, when I'm old or maybe even dead already, doctors will find a cure for him and bring him back to me. For the World Series in 2029. Every month that hope costs me all the money in the world.

Vanessa: I'm sorry.

Goosy: It doesn't bother me anymore. Sometimes I think I'm wrong. Maybe they'll never come up with a cure for those diseases. And maybe it's all just a trick to cheat gullible people out of their money. I'm too trusting, even if you might not believe it. Martin says I'm too emotional. He's probably right. You hold on to what you can. So you don't end up alone. Life and passion are one thing, but money is another, with all the responsibilities and the people you have to put up with to get it, just to spend a fraction of your time in peace.

Vanessa: I didn't mean to hurt you.

Goosy: Fighting with the boss, your everyday life and then with people like you who go around reminding everyone about every little thing they do wrong. Why can't they understand there's no other way? What's so wonderful about throwing it in our face—we know what we wanted to be. We know what we are.

Vanessa: (*On the verge of tears.*) I'm sorry, really. I'm sorry. . . .

Goosy: Well, if you wanted to see me in pain, you— (*Just then,* **Goosy** *has a heart attack and begins to fall.*) My pills . . . my—

Vanessa: What?

Goosy: My pills!

Vanessa: Where? (**Goosy** *cries out and falls.*) Wait . . . wake up . . . wake up. . . . What should I do? Come on, Goosy, stop playing around. Goosy, wait, don't look like that. Goosy. . . . (*Shouts.*) Help! (**She** *lifts* **His** *head.*) Don't go away, wait, wait, wait just a second!

ANGELS IN AMERICA
PART ONE: MILLENNIUM APPROACHES
BY TONY KUSHNER

In this part of the play, HARPER *is going crazy trying to understand the odd behavior of* HER *husband,* JOE, *whom* SHE *suspects of being gay. In the following scene,* JOE *comes home late one night, and* HARPER *finally confronts* HIM *with* HER *suspicions. Both* HARPER *and* JOE *are Mormons who have recently moved from Utah to Brooklyn, where* JOE *has taken a job as chief clerk for one of the Federal Appeals Court judges.*

HARPER: Where were you?

JOE: Out.

HARPER: Where?

JOE: Just out. Thinking.

HARPER: It's late.

JOE: I had a lot to think about.

HARPER: I burned dinner.

JOE: Sorry.

HARPER: Not my dinner. My dinner was fine. Your dinner. I put it back in the oven and turned everything up as high as it could go and I watched till it burned black. It's still hot. Very hot. Want it?

JOE: You didn't have to do that.

HARPER: I know. It just seemed like the kind of thing a mentally deranged sex-starved pill-popping housewife would do.

JOE: Uh huh.

HARPER: So I did it. Who knows anymore what I have to do?

JOE: How many pills?

HARPER: A bunch. Don't change the subject.

JOE: I won't talk to you when you . . .

HARPER: No. No. Don't do that! I'm . . . I'm fine, pills are not the problem, not our problem. I WANT TO KNOW WHERE YOU'VE BEEN! I WANT TO KNOW WHAT'S GOING ON!

JOE: Going on with what? The job?

HARPER: Not the job.

JOE: I said I need more time.

HARPER: Not the job!

JOE: Mr. Cohn, I talked to him on the phone, he said I had to hurry . . .

HARPER: Not the . . .

JOE: But I can't get you to talk sensibly about anything so . . .

Harper: SHUT UP!

Joe: Then what?

Harper: Stick to the subject.

Joe: I don't know what that is. You have something you want to ask me? Go.

Harper: I . . . can't. I'm scared of you.

Joe: I'm tired, I'm going to bed.

Harper: Tell me without making me ask. Please.

Joe: This is crazy, I'm not . . .

Harper: When you come through the door at night your face is never exactly the way I remembered it. I get surprised by something . . . mean and hard about the way you look. Even the weight of you in the bed at night, the way you breathe in your sleep seems unfamiliar. You terrify me.

Joe: (*Cold.*) I know who you are.

Harper: Yes. I'm the enemy. That's easy. That doesn't change. You think you're the only one who hates sex; I do; I hate it with you; I do. I dream that you batter away at me till all my joints come apart, like wax, and I fall into pieces. It's like a punishment. It was wrong of me to marry you. I knew you . . . (**She** *stops herself.*) It's a sin, and it's killing us both.

Joe: I can always tell when you've taken pills because it makes you red-faced and sweaty and frankly that's very often why I don't want to . . .

Harper: Because . . .

Joe: Well, you aren't pretty. Not like this.

HARPER: I have something to ask you.

JOE: Then ASK! ASK! What in hell are you.

HARPER: Are you a homo? (*Pause.*) Are you? If you try to walk out right now I'll put your dinner back in the oven and turn it up so high the whole building will fill with smoke and everyone in it will asphyxiate. So help me God I will. Now answer the question.

JOE: What if I . . . (*Small pause.*)

HARPER: Then tell me, please. And we'll see.

JOE: No. I'm not. I don't see what difference it makes . . . I think we ought to pray. Ask God for help. Ask him together . . .

HARPER: God won't talk to me. I have to make up people to talk to me.

JOE: You have to keep asking.

HARPER: I forgot the question. Oh, yeah. God, is my husband a . . .

JOE: (*Scary.*) Stop it. Stop it. I'm warning you. Does it make any difference? That I might be one thing deep within, no matter how wrong or ugly that thing is, so long as I have fought, with everything I have, to kill it. What do you want from me? What do you want from me, Harper? More than that? For God's sake, there's nothing left, I'm a shell. There's nothing left to kill. As long as my behavior is what I know it has to be. Decent. Correct. That alone in the eyes of God.

HARPER: No, no, not that, that's Utah talk, Mormon talk, I hate it, Joe, tell me, say it . . .

Joe: All I will say is that I'm a very good man who has worked very hard to become good and you want to destroy that. You want to destroy me, but I am not going to let you do that. (*Pause.*)

Harper: I'm going to have a baby.

Joe: Liar.

Harper: You liar. A baby born addicted to pills. A baby who does not dream but who hallucinates, who stares up at us with big mirror eyes and who does not know who we are. (*Pause.*)

Joe: Are you really . . .

Harper: No. Yes. No. Yes. Get away from me. Now we both have a secret.

CONVIVENCIA
BY R. N. SANDBERG

A stone gateway in the Jewish section of the city. Evening is falling. Footsteps are heard—someone running in the shadows. The steps stop but there's heavy breathing. The breathing slows. From off, humming: YTZHA, *a sturdy girl of fourteen, enters carrying a lit candle.* SHE *wears a yellow cap and yellow robe with a "badge" on it, marking her as a Jew.* SHE *comes to the stone gateway, stops, kisses* HER *fingertips and touches them to the mezuzah on the gateway.* SHE *then passes through the gate. The light from* HER *candle reveals a menorah, set in the stone arch.* SHE *prays before the menorah.*

YTZHA: Blessed art Thou, Lord our God, King of the Universe, who has commanded us to kindle the lights. (SHE *begins to light the candles. As* SHE *does so,* SHE *stops and listens.* SHE *hears something.* SHE *calls into the distance, away from the house.*) Father? Father, is that you?? (SHE *gets no response.* SHE *senses something behind* HER *in the shadows.* SHE *turns quickly.*) What are you doing? Why are you hiding there? (MA'IL, HIS *face and clothes smudged with dirt and soot, comes out of the shadows.*)

MA'IL: Please.

YTZHA: Are you Ahkmed's son? Have you come about the fish? My father—

Ma'il: No, please, be quiet.

Ytzha: Why? What's wrong? Why are you so frightened?

Ma'il: Help me.

Ytzha: I . . . come back at dusk tomorrow. My father—

Ma'il: No.

Ytzha: It's the Sabbath. There's nothing we can do tonight.

Ma'il: I can't leave.

Ytzha: You have to.

Ma'il: I can't. (*Awkwardly,* **Ma'il** *grabs the knife from beside the menorah.* **He** *thrusts it out in* **His** *shaking hand.*)

Ytzha: Oh God. (**She** *stays very still. With the knife nervously quaking in* **His** *hand,* **He** *motions to the menorah.*)

Ma'il: Blow the candles out.

Ytzha: You know I can't.

Ma'il: Blow them out.

Ytzha: It's Shabbat. You know our law. No work on the Sabbath. (**They** *are both shaking.*)

Ma'il: I know your law. Blow them out.

Ytzha: No. (**She** *seems immovable.* **Ma'il** *begins blowing out the candles himself.*)

Ma'il: No wonder we have to teach your children.

Ytzha: You teach us because we pay. And your prophet Muhammad would have had no Qur'an if it weren't for our Torah, so you learn from us, too. (**Ma'il** *glances nervously towards the house.*)

Ma'il: That's enough. Someone will hear.

Ytzha: What do you want?

Ma'il: Quiet.

Ytzha: Why are you here? Why aren't you in your part of the city?

Ma'il: Enough, I said.

Ytzha: Have the Christians come?

Ma'il: If you speak again, I'll . . . I'll cut out your tongue. I've ripped them from peacocks with one slice. I'll do the same to you. (**Ma'il** *brandishes the knife at* **Her** *but* **His** *hand is shaking and* **He** *almost drops it.* **Ytzha** *stifles a laugh.*)

Ytzha: You've never cut off a peacock's tongue. Their beaks are sharp, and you hold that like a ball of soap. Anyway, it's a dull thing for scraping wax. It'd take you an hour of sawing to cut out my tongue. My father says respect the Muslims; they're great thinkers. He should meet you.

(*Deflated,* **Ma'il** *slumps against the archway.* **Ytzha** *watches* **Him** *for a moment.*)

Has something terrible happened? I saw smoke all afternoon and wondered if it was the Christians. After seven hundred years, to have come back. Has there been fighting? Have you been in a battle? A battle must be very exciting. If you like excitement. . . . Well, I guess I'm going to go in now.

Ma'il: Don't.

Ytzha: Why? I can talk to myself inside.

Ma'il: Stay for a bit.

Ytzha: Why should I?

Ma'il: You . . . you probably shouldn't.

Ytzha: Yes, well, I think my father'd prefer I go in. He gets upset when I'm gone for more than five minutes.

Ma'il: He does?

Ytzha: He's got a horrible temper, too. He's sitting right by the door. To hear any troubles in the street. If he knew I were talking to you . . . if he knew you were here by our house . . . you should see the knife he has. I've seen him slit open stomachs and empty innards just like that.

Ma'il: No.

Ytzha: In fact, maybe I should call him since you tried to threaten me. (**Ma'il** *grabs* **Her** *and holds* **Her** *tightly.*)

Ma'il: Don't.

Ytzha: I'm sorry. I was joking. You've nothing to fear. He's . . . He won't come out. (**Ma'il** *slides to the ground,* **His** *back against the gate.* **Ma'il**'*s head sinks down on* **His** *chest. The knife falls from* **His** *hand and clinks on the ground. Slowly,* **Ytzha** *moves to* **Ma'il** *and takes the knife.* **She** *stands over* **Him**, *holding the knife easily in* **Her** *hand, circling.*)

Ytzha: I've never touched a peacock, but I've gutted my share of fish. (**She** *laughs softly as* **She** *continues to circle, exhilarated. The darkness begins to envelop* **Them**.)

PILGRIMS MUSA AND SHERI IN THE NEW WORLD
BY YUSSEF EL GUINDI

MUSA *and* SHERI *fall in love in this opening scene,* SHE *from the world of "loose" morals and social freedom of the West and* HE *from the strictly conservative Muslim Mideast. But* THEIR *mutual attraction to each other overrides* THEIR *cultural and religious differences, and makes* THEIR *encounter something more than a simple story of momentary lust and fatal attraction. Their relationship is at times very comic and at other times very touching; the characters' sincerity with each other creates a relationship that is precious, fragile, and charmingly human. The setting is* MUSA's *drab and impoverished New York City flat at two in the morning, dimly lighted by the glow of a streetlamp. A bed, a mattress on the floor, a table and some chairs. Voices are heard offstage as the couple reach the top of the stairs.*

MUSA: (*Offstage, accent.*) One more flight.

SHERI: (*Offstage.*) Geez. For a three-story walk-up it feels like I'm climbing a high-rise. You must have the penthouse, huh.

MUSA: (*Offstage.*) Good exercise.

SHERI: (*Offstage.*) Not after eight hours on my feet. You've got it lucky, you sit on your tush all night. (*The sound of a key being inserted. The door opens.* **Musa** *and* **Sheri** *enter.* **Sheri** *wears a waitress outfit.*)

Musa: Here we are. Home. My little kingdom. (*There is the muffled sound of a door slamming from the apartment above.* **Musa** *briefly looks up.*)

Sheri: This is too sad. My panting like this.

Musa: You smoke?

Sheri: I gave it up.

Musa: I have hookah.

Sheri: What's that? (**He** *hits the light switch. But no light.*)

Musa: Damn. I get fuse. Wait a moment. (**Musa** *walks to the fuse box.* **Sheri** *looks around.*)

Sheri: (*Half to herself.*) Kingdom, huh?

Musa: What?

Sheri: Nice place.

Musa: I finish in one moment. (**Sheri** *sits.* **She** *grimaces. Massages the pain in* **Her** *stomach.* **Musa** *enters and heads for the light switch.*) Wiring not good here.

Sheri: At least you have the street light. It's—nice. (**Musa** *switches the light on: an overhead bulb.*) Ow. That's light alright.

Musa: I have to get lamp shade.

Sheri: I think so. Nobody looks good in that light. (*Slight beat.*) Home sweet home, huh.

Musa: It's cheap; not nice.

SHERI: It's alright.

MUSA: I sleep here, that's all. Later, when I save enough, I buy a place.

SHERI: (*Seeing the mattress.*) Who else sleeps here?

MUSA: Abdallah. He's gone. He makes the hajj.

SHERI: The what?

MUSA: Trip to Mecca. Pilgrimage.

SHERI: I know that. I saw a special on TV. People dressed in white, going around that . . .

MUSA: (*Points to calendar photo on the wall.*) Kaaba.

SHERI: Yeah. Have you done that?

MUSA: One day I will.

SHERI: (*Walks over to look at photo.*) It looks so intense. With all those people. Like Woodstock, you know. On steroids, without the music. Well, maybe not like that. But it looked like everyone was so into it. I'd love to be able to lose myself in something like that.

MUSA: Yes . . . I dream of it sometimes. (*Slight beat.*) You still want drink?

SHERI: Sure. So is your roommate coming back soon?

MUSA: (*Goes to tiny kitchen area.*) He move out when he return. The man make lots of money. Big time now. He wants bigger place. I have alcohol if you want.

SHERI: Great. That's what I thought you meant.

MUSA: Scotch.

Sheri: I'll take it.

Musa: This Somali friend, he give me Johnny Walker as payment after I help him take merchandise across bridge a few times. Say he not believe in money between friends.

Sheri: That's a good one. I must remember that.

Musa: (*Getting the bottle, pouring drinks.*) I say, I have no problem getting money from friend. He say, no no, money is the devil, and a good friend would not bring the devil into a friend's life. I say, I have strong faith, give me this devil, I will fight it. He say, better not risk it.

Sheri: Alcohol is okay though.

Musa: I say, so you corrupt me with drink? He say now you test your faith with drink. Money is like invisible evil. But drink, you know what it is. I give you good way to prove your faith.

Sheri: Some friend.

Musa: You want ice? Water?

Sheri: Nothing. Just like that.

Musa: I say, so am I not supposed to drink this gift? Leave it as temptation? Ah, he says. (*Hands* **Her** *the drink.*) That is up to you. That is the point.

Sheri: A real joker. What does he do?

Musa: Sells suitcases on Broadway. I take him and his merchandise every few weeks across bridge.

Sheri: (*Toasting.*) Well: here's to temptation. And the faith to resist it.

Musa: Yes. (**They** *drink.* **She** *grimaces.*)

SHERI: Kick.

MUSA: You want water in it?

SHERI: I'm not a big scotch person.

MUSA: I have soda drink. (*Sees* **HER** *clutching* **HER** *stomach.*) You okay?

SHERI: Just something I ate. (*Regarding overhead bulb.*) You really need a lamp. Or lamp shade or something.

MUSA: I can turn it off.

SHERI: You don't have a lamp? Candles? That would soften the place up. I saw some candles in that corner store window.

MUSA: We try with just kitchen light. (**HE** *goes to turn off overhead lamp.*)

SHERI: He's open kinda late, isn't he? For this neighborhood?

MUSA: He not very good man. Stays open for junkies. He knows they want things at night. I say, why you do that? You Muslim. This is not good. (*Turns on kitchen light.*) He say nothing. Says it's business. (*Goes into the bathroom.*)

SHERI: Well, they don't have to buy his stuff. If he wants to stay open, let him.

MUSA: But it's not right. Not being a good Muslim. (**HE** *turns on the bathroom light. With this new lighting—including the street light—***THEIR** *faces will still be clearly visible.*)

SHERI: Let he who is without sin cast the first stone.

MUSA: What?

SHERI: We're all sinners.

Musa: But some sins are obvious. You can say no.

Sheri: Like scotch?

Musa: This is a weakness. God understands weakness.

Sheri: Sounds like a slippery slope to me.

Musa: Slippery slope?

Sheri: Little weaknesses? Adding up?

Musa: Yes.

Sheri: (*Regarding new light.*) Better. Now I won't feel like I've walked into an interrogation room or something. Where all this bad skin (*Touches* **Her** *cheeks.*) gets shown up.

Musa: You have nice skin.

Sheri: Now it's more like I'm in a setting for a murder mystery or something, with these shadows. Very moody.

Musa: Is okay?

Sheri: Someone in a trench coat would fit right in, if he knocked on the door. And maybe a lady in the shadows blowing smoke rings. (**They** *look at each other.*) Speaking of which, are you like—safe? Should I be worried?

Musa: About what?

Sheri: You know—with me in your apartment—and with this now looking like a set for a movie where the lady you see in the first few minutes gets taken out by the man she shouldn't have gone so casually up to his apartment with. I mean—what kind of good girl accepts an invitation for a drink at two a.m. From a guy she's just met a couple of times.

MUSA: I give you lift three, four times. We are night birds, you and me. This is when we wake up.

SHERI: Yeah, and you shouldn't be playing hooky; you should be out there earning money.

MUSA: I make up for it tomorrow. This is the afternoon for us. This is when we work; and you have just finished.

SHERI: So I don't come off looking quite as . . . can still come off as the good girl, huh? At two a.m. Drinking scotch. With somebody I don't know so well.

MUSA: You like mystery books? I learn English by reading crime books. (*Goes to a small pile of books by* HIS *bed; has trouble pronouncing authors' names.*) Raymond Chandler. Dashiell Hammett. One good thing about corner store is he has box full of books for a dollar. Crime is easy way to learn. And yes: you could be girl in book like this. Sometimes, in my taxi, I pretend I am like American tough guy, investigating something.

SHERI: (*Picks up book.*) What's this one?

MUSA: Oh. Not mystery. This is translation of Qur'an.

SHERI: A holy book, right?

MUSA: I learn English also this way too, since I know original.

SHERI: (*Reading from random passage.*) "Allah knows what the heavens and the earth contain. If three men talk in secret together, He is their fourth; if four, He is their fifth; if five, He is their sixth; whether fewer or more, wherever they be, He is with them."

MUSA: (*Wanting to take Qur'an from* HER.) Maybe this is not the time.

Sheri: (*Holding onto the Qu'ran.*) This is a kind of mystery book too, right?

Musa: Not really.

Sheri: It's a whodunit, isn't it?

Musa: We know who done it: God.

Sheri: Why is it titled "She Who Pleaded"?

Musa: It is the name of the Sutra.

Sheri: What?

Musa: Chapter. The title of the chapter.

Sheri: We, no, we don't know who done it. If you think of God as the top cop, and we're like the sinners being investigated. And maybe the angels are like the people he sends down to investigate our deeds. Then it is a kinda mystery.

Musa: (*Tries to take the book, but* **She** *holds on to it.*) He knows everything, he doesn't need to investigate.

Sheri: I don't know, people can get pretty sneaky.

Musa: He knows sneaky.

Sheri: Some things might slip by. He's a busy guy.

Musa: This is interesting idea but not true.

Sheri: How do you know?

Musa: (*Tries to get the book again.*) You just read passage that say He is always here.

Sheri: Oh. Right. But still, I think you could make a good case for God being like the top detective in the sky. And we're like—the people in a mystery being investigated, for possible involvement in crap. Like when people get nasty with each other. Or invite people up to their apartments with bad intentions.

Musa: (*Taking the book from* **Her**.) We stop talking about God.

Sheri: Why?

Musa: Because—I want to relax.

Sheri: God doesn't relax you?

Musa: We have talked of God enough.

Sheri: But I love these kind of talks. You must get them in your taxi at night. The night shift's so cool because people open up and talk about things they wouldn't have time for, or feel too shy about in the day. And God is like right up there on my five top things to talk about. If you talk of God during the day, people think you're a religious nut.

Musa: You religious?

Sheri: I have aspirations . . . get distracted. Life happens. And then who has time to think about anything.

Musa: What is other four things you like to talk about? We pick one of those instead.

Sheri: Trust me, God is the lightest subject of the bunch.

Musa: Tell me about other four; we talk about those instead.

Sheri: Well there's my weight. Right after God. Though the weight thing's more a private conversation I have with myself. I sometimes think just thinking about my weight is the issue, you know, like some private thoughts actually come with calories?

Like there are fat thoughts, and thin thoughts. And if I stopped with the heavy thoughts, I would physically be lighter.

Musa: Why you think about weight? You are thin.

Sheri: That's very kind of you, but I'm not.

Musa: Where is this weight? I don't see it.

Sheri: That's—thank you. It's there. You just can't see it under the shirt.

Musa: You are skinny. Too much skinny. You must eat more.

Sheri: Oh that's—you are like picking the line I most fantasize about hearing.

Musa: I am serious, any thinner and you need to go to hospital.

Sheri: I wish. Okay, let's stop there while you're doing good.

Musa: Show me. So I understand when women talk about weight, I know maybe they are crazy instead.

Sheri: Alright. What are these? (*Partially lifts shirt or blouse and pinches skin.*) And before you say "love handles," they're not. These are more like thick, rubber escalator hand rails.

Musa: This you call fat?

Sheri: And just like escalator rubber, it just keeps circulating; even when you think you've lost the fat, here it is again.

Musa: This is normal weight; and beautiful.

Sheri: You know, I actually feel giddy hearing you say that.

Musa: Why you shy from what makes you stand out? (**His** *hand touches* **Her** *waist.*)

SHERI: Now, you see. That was a poor choice of words; and you were doing so good.

MUSA: What you mean? This is lovely. And very soft. And lucky you, you go to sleep with it every night. (**HIS** *hand stays on* **HER** *waist, as* **HE** *gently, a little shyly, runs* **HIS** *hand across* **HER** *waist, stomach. Without the context/excuse of the conversation continuing, the touching suddenly feels more pointed, awkward.* **HE** *stops. Slight beat.*)

SHERI: So you never answered my question.

MUSA: About what?

SHERI: Are you safe?

MUSA: What you mean?

SHERI: You know—if you were in my shoes, would you like, run away?

MUSA: Why?

SHERI: Because. I don't know you. And maybe you should be concerned about me. I'm a stranger too. I could be anyone.

MUSA: I like strangers. I give rides to them every day.

SHERI: And I serve them. Doesn't mean I'd invite them over for a drink.

MUSA: So you dangerous? You like woman in my books? Big trouble? "Help me, Mister. I'm in trouble. I think someone's following me."

SHERI: Yeah, I am being followed.

MUSA: Who by?

SHERI: You.

IN THE SHAPE OF
A WOMAN
BY TAMMY RYAN

Of all the most celebrated examples of the conflict between church and state, perhaps none is more famous than that of JOAN OF ARC *in the fourteenth century. Although* JOAN *was condemned to be burned at the stake for heresy by a French ecclesiastical court, the churchmen were plainly in the power of the English occupying forces. They wanted to kill* JOAN *because of* HER *ability to galvanize the French army against them, but in executing* HER *they only created a martyr whose fame and example still continue to inspire millions today. The church-state conflict is boldly expressed in this scene in a modern version of the story; the actors' choices become especially interesting at the very end, where* JOAN'*s resolve begins to break down, begging* CAUCHON *to return* HER *ring.*

CAUCHON: This inquiry confirms our original suspicions and so we begin our examination of this woman, on all she has said, done and knows. (*To* JOAN *with a brief smile.*) Joan, for the quicker ending of this trial and the unburdening of your conscience, swear to tell the truth.

JOAN: (SHE *doesn't answer immediately.*) No.

CAUCHON: Maybe you didn't understand us. We command you to swear on the Gospel that you will speak the truth—

JOAN: I don't know what you're going to ask me.

CAUCHON: We'll ask you what you know, about your background and your revelations and about all matters concerning the faith.

JOAN: You might ask me something I won't tell you.

CAUCHON: If you don't take the oath, we'll have to presume you're not telling us the truth.

JOAN: I can't control what you're going to presume.

CAUCHON: We can't proceed with this interrogation until you swear to tell the truth about everything we will ask you.

JOAN: Concerning my mother and father and what I've done since I've taken the road to France, I'll happily swear. But concerning my revelations from God, I've never revealed them to anyone except the true King, Charles of France, and I won't reveal them to you just to save my neck, for what came to me in secret counsel is for my King alone.

CAUCHON: We are your judges in this case, it is to us, you must truthfully confess all that you know.

JOAN: If you are to judge me, then I demand to have an equal number of judges from the French side.

CAUCHON: We are churchmen, we have no allegiances to particular parties.

JOAN: If you are churchmen, I demand to hear Mass.

CAUCHON: Denied, because of your crimes and the impropriety of the garments to which you cling.

JOAN: If you are a churchman, then hear my confession.

CAUCHON: Take the oath and we'll have your confession here.

JOAN: Are you priest or judge?

CAUCHON: In this case, I am both. Swear.

JOAN: (*Kneels, with both hands on the missal.*) I swear to answer truthfully, but not on everything I know.

CAUCHON: Before we go further, I want this to be perfectly clear: you will not try to leave the prison we've assigned to you in this castle, without our permission, on pain of the crime of heresy.

JOAN: It's not likely I'd escape since you keep me chained to my bed in irons. If this is a church prison, I wouldn't be chained like this and I'd have women guards.

CAUCHON: You have escaped before.

JOAN: It's true, and I wish to escape even now.

CAUCHON: Well, we don't wish it. We expressly forbid it.

JOAN: You can't forbid it. It is the right of every prisoner to escape.

CAUCHON: And so it is the right of every judge to prevent that escape.

JOAN: I DEMAND TO HAVE WOMEN GUARDS!

CAUCHON: We'll conclude these proceedings until tomorrow.

JOAN: I SHOULD BE IN A CHURCH PRISON!

CAUCHON: When we will enjoin the said Joan to take our oath again.

JOAN: I SHOULD HAVE SOMEONE TO ADVISE ME!

CAUCHON: You will appear before us tomorrow at eight o'clock in morning in the Ornament Room in the Great Hall of the Castle of Rouen, and we will begin again.

JOAN: WAIT, BISHOP! You have something of mine. A ring you took from me. I want it back.

CAUCHON: Why, does it have some magic in it to help you escape?

JOAN: It was just a ring my mother gave me.

CAUCHON: What's it made of?

JOAN: I don't know whether it is gold or brass. It has three crosses on it, and the words: Jesu Maria. Please.

CAUCHON: No.

SOME PEOPLE HAVE ALL THE LUCK

BY CÁNDIDO TIRADO

In this charming contemporary fantasy, Carlos *has been considering suicide on account of* His *broken dreams of a happy family, when* He *confronts* Damasia, *a spirit seeking a body for* Her *next incarnation. Beneath the fantasy, however, lie the unspoken yearnings that both cherish for a better life than what they've* They've *just had in this,* Their *present one. The scene brings the material, everyday world into a dialogue with the unseen, spiritual world; both characters realize at the end the common human longings, hopes, and challenges that* They *share.*

Carlos: Nice weather we're having.

Damasia: Yeah, for a funeral. (He *laughs.* She *looks at* Him *sharply.* He *stops laughing.*) I hate the rain.

Carlos: I hate it, too.

Damasia: You just called it nice.

Carlos: Well . . . Sometimes I like it and sometimes I don't.

Damasia: And how do you feel about it now?

Carlos: Now?

DAMASIA: Now!

CARLOS: I . . . I don't know.

DAMASIA: Do you feel uncomfortable?

CARLOS: Why? Just because you're a spirit?

DAMASIA: Do you have something against spirits?

CARLOS: No. No. I wish I was one.

DAMASIA: Yeah, I forgot. (*Pause.*) Actually, it isn't that bad being a spirit. If it wasn't for the fact that you had to be dead, I would be able to live with it. I mean, I could appear and disappear. Walk through walls. Travel for free. I don't have to worry about gaining weight.

CARLOS: It sounds like fun.

DAMASIA: It gets lonely sometimes. You can't start a conversation without putting someone into shock. You're the first person I've talked to since. . . . Excuse me, I have to get ready for an interview. (**SHE** *exits to the bedroom.*)

CARLOS: Job . . . Job interview?

DAMASIA: (*From the bedroom.*) Body interview.

CARLOS: (*As if understanding.*) Oh!

DAMASIA: A body is like a shoe. You need the right fit. Not too tight, not too loose.

CARLOS: Then, spirits are like feet.

DAMASIA: Clean ones. Just kidding. See, I go all over the world interviewing possible bodies to take over. And I think I found the right one in a Brooklyn hospital. Coma! I hope she doesn't have a Brooklyn accent. Today I take over it. (**She** *enters wearing a silky white dress.*) This life is going to be different. I'm going for it all. I'm going to be number one. It's going to be up, up and up. Nothing is going to keep me down. (*The funeral march is heard.*) I hate that depressing music. (**She** *bangs on the heating pipe.* **She** *goes to the table, sits, and begins to put* **Her** *white stockings on.* **She** *notices* **Carlos** *looking at* **Her** *and* **She** *gives* **Him** **Her** *back.*) Could you believe they only give you three months to find a body?

Carlos: There should be a lot of bodies around.

Damasia: Are you out of your mind? Do you realize how much damage people do to their bodies? The greasy food they eat! Do you exercise?

Carlos: No.

Damasia: I didn't think so. Most people who exercise only look good on the outside. Their insides are rotting away. Even the worms stay away from them if you know what I mean.

Carlos: I didn't think about that.

Damasia: (**She** *looks at herself in the mirror.* **Carlos** *takes out a set of frames and looks at them.*) There's only one thing I don't like about being a spirit. You can only wear white. I never liked white. It makes me look fat. And another thing, we can't see ourselves in the mirror. (*Walks over to* **Carlos.**) Well, how do I look? (**He** *hides the picture frames.*) Why are you hiding those pictures from me?

Carlos: What pictures?

Damasia: Those behind your back.

Carlos: No . . . No reason.

Damasia: Can I see them?

Carlos: No.

Damasia: Why not?

Carlos: It's a personal thing.

Damasia: Yeah, sure. Naked women, right?

Carlos: (*Hurt by insinuation.*) They are not naked women.

Damasia: Naked men?

Carlos: Of course not.

Damasia: Damn! Who are they then?

Carlos: Nobody.

Damasia: He reads comic books. He has naked women in frames.

Carlos: It's my wife and kids.

Damasia: (*Surprised.*) You're married? And with kids? I don't believe it. I mean, you don't look like the type. Let me see them.

Carlos: No.

Damasia: Please, I love kids. I always dreamed of having a house full of kids. I'd come home after working all day and my husband would have them cleaned and ready for supper. I admire people with kids. It's a great achievement.

Carlos: Okay, but don't say how cute they are.

Damasia: I won't. I promise. (**He** *gives* **Her** *the frames.* **Her** *excitement turns to bafflement. The frames are empty.* **She** *looks at them from different angles.* **She** *even puts* **Her** *hand through them.*) What happened to the pictures?

Carlos: Is something wrong?

Damasia: Where are the kids?

Carlos: Right there.

Damasia: Where? I don't see them.

Carlos: Just because you don't see them it doesn't mean they aren't there. I didn't see you and you were here.

Damasia: Oh. They are dead. I'm sorry.

Carlos: No. In this frame is the woman that would've been my wife. Sandra. And my son Carlitos and my daughter Sandrita are in this one.

Damasia: Oh, I see. These are the kids you would've had.

Carlos: Yeah.

Damasia: So, you and Sandra separated?

Carlos: Yeah, but I took the kids.

Damasia: The kids you would've had?

Carlos: That's what I said.

Damasia: I'm just trying to get the story straight. . . . They would've been cute.

Carlos: I told you not to say that.

Damasia: I couldn't help it.

Carlos: They are cute. The boy is nothing like me. He's a winner. Everybody want to be his friend. The girls don't ever leave him alone. . . . Every Sunday I took them to the park. They love the swing. . . . They love to swing real high. I'd push them higher and higher. . . . And when they swung down they said, Papi, papi, I got a piece of sky for you. (*Pause.* **He** *looks out the window, trying not to cry.*) Now, they're ashamed of me. They think I'm a loser.

DAMASIA: They don't think that.

CARLOS: How do you know?

DAMASIA: Kids don't think like we do.

CARLOS: I couldn't even propose to their mother.

DAMASIA: It's not easy to ask someone to marry you.

CARLOS: I didn't even ask her out on a date.

DAMASIA: But you and Sandra had a relationship?

CARLOS: It was a secret love.

DAMASIA: How romantic. Nobody knew.

CARLOS: Even Sandra didn't know.

DAMASIA: So, you broke off with Sandra before she knew she was going out with you?

CARLOS: (*Starts crying.*) Can you believe it?

DAMASIA: And that's why you want to kill yourself?

CARLOS: She threw my sandwich away. Every day I used to leave her a sandwich on her desk. She didn't know it was me. She used to eat them . . . And yesterday without a clue she threw my heart-shaped sandwich in the garbage can.

DAMASIA: She must've had a big lunch.

CARLOS: It was morning.

DAMASIA: There it is. She had a big breakfast.

Carlos: She never ate breakfast. I can't live without her. I want to die.

Damasia: I know how you feel.

Carlos: How could you know?

Damasia: The pain becomes a sword across your chest. Your chest wants to explode. You want to stab yourself a thousand times so it could alleviate the pain. You decide to take your life.

Carlos: Yeah, that's it. How did you know?

Damasia: That's how I felt when I didn't get the promotion to become president of that company I slaved for so many years. You'll get over it.

Carlos: I'm sorry for laying all this on you.

Damasia: You have nothing to be sorry about . . . Wow! It's so embarrassing.

Carlos: What?

Damasia: The nature of our meeting. You want to kill yourself and I'm already. . . . Never mind. Excuse me.

GOLDEN CHILD
BY DAVID HENRY HWANG

The cultural tension in China between tradition and modernity is not a new theme, nor is it a societal tension particular only to China. Like many societies struggling to adapt to the global age, the collision between Eastern and Western value systems creates awkward situations on many social levels, including the personal level between a man and his wife. The play is set in China circa 1918 and deals with the conflict between tradition and change as depicted in one man's family. TIENG-BIN is a wealthy landowner with three wives, but HE has been away from China, living in the Philippines for three years on business, and has just returned. This scene follows a homecoming dinner with HIS favorite wife, ELING, who playfully mocks HIS recent adoption of modernized "Christian" values while HE has been living in Manila.

ELING: You shouldn't have praised me so much in front of the other wives. Second Wife will be fuming for weeks.

TIENG-BIN: But—just looking at you across the dinner table . . .

ELING: Are you going to make me blush again?

TIENG-BIN: I would never have believed my eyes could give me so much pleasure.

ELING: Just your eyes? What about your other senses?

Tieng-Bin: Well, you see, I thought I'd try out this new form of Western self-restraint.

Eling: What kind of ridiculous—? (**She** *reaches for* **Him**. **He** *pulls away*.)

Tieng-Bin: I'm restricting my intake of physical pleasures.

Eling: By now, your pleasure should be just about ready to explode.

Tieng-Bin: I've been living among the Christians, remember?

Eling: What does that have to do—?

Tieng-Bin: They consider abstinence a great virtue.

Eling: Says who? I hear white men stuff money into their pockets and meat down their thick throats.

Tieng-Bin: Don't be so close-minded—

Eling: Oh? Am I not—what?—*modern* enough for you? You already insulted my feet tonight.

Tieng-Bin: I'm sorry. That was just a slip of the tongue.

Eling: Where I come from, insults always get punished. (*Keeping* **Her** *back to* **Him**, **She** *crosses to the phonograph, sashaying seductively as* **She** *walks*.) So—you only want to watch? Like a good Christian? You say you are a modern man who wants a modern wife? (**Eling** *removes* **Her** *robe, revealing Western lingerie*.)

Tieng-Bin: Where did you get that outfit?

Eling: From the catalog. I've been so busy improving myself. (*Pause*.) I like being modern, too. I like my new phonograph player. (*Begins to dance to the music, keeping* **Her** *back to* **Him**.) I like this *Traviata*. It fills me with feelings. Modern feelings.

Delicious feelings of . . . power. (**TIENG-BIN** *rises to* **HIS** *feet, starts toward* **HER**.) No, no, no. Self-denial. Like a good Christian.

TIENG-BIN: Eling. . . .

ELING: I'm your slave, remember? I can only obey your wishes. (**ELING** *eludes* **HIM**.)

TIENG-BIN: What are you—? You're going to kill me! . . .

ELING: You must be able to hold out longer than that, Honored Husband.

TIENG-BIN: I haven't touched a woman in three years!

ELING: You expect me to believe that? The prostitutes in Manila must be for shit.

TIENG-BIN: That's enough!

ELING: My lord and master . . . Sit!

TIENG-BIN: Eling!

ELING: Now, be modern. Sit! You wait for me to come to you. (*Pause.*) When you're away, I would put this on and imagine your face as you lowered the straps from my shoulders . . .

TIENG-BIN: Now, you don't have to imagine any longer . . .

ELING: Not yet. Will you please struggle for me a little longer?

TIENG-BIN: But . . . why?

ELING: I don't know. It lets me know you care. That you suffer for me . . . like I suffer for you.

TIENG-BIN: Don't you believe that I want to spend every night here with you?

ELING: Yes, but you have your duty to the other wives.

TIENG-BIN: Eling . . . you are the first woman I was ever able to choose for myself . . . and you will be the last.

ELING: Now, if you like, you may touch me. (**HE** *kisses* **HER**.) *You know I'm going to pay for every one of those kisses.*

TIENG-BIN: What are you—?

ELING: When you're away, Second Wife bursts into my room whenever she feels like it, breaks—

TIENG-BIN: Eling, please. At least here, let's not talk about the others. I want to think only of you—as if you were my only wife.

ELING: That sounds so naughty.

TIENG-BIN: You're the one person from whom I want to have no secrets. This is my fantasy: that we will speak only words that are true.

ELING: Then can I tell you my secret? (*Pause.*) I like it. That you come to me—that you look at me different from the other wives . . . I like it.

TIENG-BIN: Then look back at me. Don't avert your gaze, but look me straight in the eye. Watch me, watching you.

LYNETTE AT 3 A.M.
BY JANE ANDERSON

Tossing and turning in bed and unable to sleep, LYNETTE *has thought* SHE *heard a gunshot from somewhere in the building. Moments later, apparently after* SHE *has fallen asleep,* ESTABAN, *a young Latino man, appears in her bedroom.* HE *is barefoot and dressed in a white T-shirt and white pants.* LYNETTE *stares at him. Is* SHE *dreaming? Or having a supernatural out-of-body experience with a recently departed soul?*

ESTABAN: Hello. My name is Estaban. I'm from the apartment below. I just died.

LYNETTE: Oh my God.

ESTABAN: I am sorry to disturb you. I have to pass through so I can go . . . (HE *points up.*) . . . to above.

LYNETTE: Was this like a few minutes ago this happened?

ESTABAN: Yes.

LYNETTE: I thought I heard a gun. Was that you?

ESTABAN: Yes.

LYNETTE: You know, I knew there was something. I told Bobby. I said to him there was definitely a shot. So that was you?

ESTABAN: That was me.

LYNETTE: I was gonna call the police. Should I call the police?

ESTABAN: It doesn't matter anymore

LYNETTE: Who shot you?

ESTABAN: My brother Jorge.

LYNETTE: Oh my God, your brother?

ESTABAN: I was making love to his wife.

LYNETTE: Oh. Well. That wasn't a smart thing to be doing.

ESTABAN: It couldn't be helped. Lola and me, we fell in love when we were fifteen.

LYNETTE: Really? So this has been going on a long time then.

ESTABAN: Yes. Me and Lola, we grew up in the same village in Puerto Rico.

LYNETTE: I hear Puerto Rico is a nice place to vacation. Is it nice there?

ESTABAN: Like a paradise.

LYNETTE: I've always wanted to see the islands. But Bobby, he's not a traveler.

ESTABAN: No?

LYNETTE: But you and Lola, I want to hear about. So you met on the island, you were soul mates, go on.

ESTABAN: The first time we made love it was siesta time. We walked down the street, everyone was asleep. Everything was quiet except for the waves flipping over very soft. It was hot, just a little bit windy from the ocean. Very sexy. I took her to the shade of a vanilla bean tree. We lay down on a blanket. She opened her blouse for me and her skin, it smelled sweet just like the tree. After we made love, I cried.

LYNETTE: I do that too. I cry after Bobby and me make love. So you cry too?

ESTABAN: Oh yes. It is because when I make love, my heart leaves my body for heaven. And when it is over and my heart has to come back, it is very sad.

LYNETTE: See, my crying thing is a little different. When I make love and my heart leaves my body I'm always expecting to meet Bobby's heart outside his body. But Bobby's heart—well, Bobby has a hard time opening up, if you met his family you'd understand. His heart doesn't really leave his body, so my heart is alone out there waiting while Bobby finishes up. Below. And then he falls asleep and I'm still out there, floating and feeling very lonely. And then I cry and wake Bobby up and he gets annoyed. Which is not to say that I don't get a lot of other things from him.

ESTABAN: Yes?

LYNETTE: So how come Lola didn't marry you?

ESTABAN: Her parents said, "Lola, marry Jorge he make better money than Estaban."

LYNETTE: Aw, that's not fair.

ESTABAN: That is life. Jorge, he runs a car service to the airport. I been working for him. Olmos Limo.

LYNETTE: I hate to fly. I see my own death when I fly.

ESTABAN: See, when I drive someone to the airport I always say before they get out "have a safe trip, God bless." Not one of my passengers ever died in a plane crash. It's part of the service.

LYNETTE: That's nice. (*A beat.*) So do you know where you're going? Is anyone gonna be meeting you, like do you have grandparents or anyone who're gonna take you over to the other side?

ESTABAN: No, all my family's still alive.

LYNETTE: Are you Catholic?

ESTABAN: Yeah, I grew up with that.

LYNETTE: Do you think the Virgin Mary will be there?

ESTABAN: I don't know.

LYNETTE: Did you go through a tunnel and see a white light?

ESTABAN: No. I haven't even left the building yet.

LYNETTE: Are you scared?

ESTABAN: What's to be scared? It's nature. Everything dies. Chickens and dogs and pussy cats and movie stars and cockroaches, and grandmommies and guys like me who drive people to the airport. We all gotta do it. So how can something that everybody has to do be so bad?

LYNETTE: But you think there's something to go to? You think there's something else?

ESTABAN: Sure, why not?

LYNETTE: Bobby says all that stuff is bullshit, that when you die you die.

ESTABAN: Oh man, don't listen to him. How can a guy who can't make good love know anything about the afterlife? Geez, no wonder you're such a scared lady.

LYNETTE: I didn't paint a fair picture. He's a very good person.

ESTABAN: What's your name?

LYNETTE: Lynette.

ESTABAN: Ay, Lynetta, Lynetta. *Tu eres muy amable y muy hermosa. Deseo que te pudiera besarte y tener tus cenos en mis manos como si fueran frutas perfectas, desmasiados bellas para comer.*

FROM EVERY
MOUNTAINSIDE
BY MAX BUSH

Brutally persecuted and suppressed by the government since the mid-1990s, disciples of Falun Dafa (or Falun Gong) still practice this spiritual discipline within and outside of mainland China. Derived from ancient Buddhist and Taoist practices and teachings, the Falun Dafa is a series of slow-moving meditation exercises similar to the more familiar discipline of Tai Chi. Both aim to strengthen health and bring about spiritual enlightenment. In this scene, SUSAN *attempts to teach* MATT *about the movement meditation that* SHE *and* HER *parents have practiced for years, and to enlist* HIS *support for* HER *protest against the Yahoo corporation for having "informed" the government of the names of Chinese citizens using Yahoo's Internet services. The Chinese government, as* SUSAN *explains, has "disappeared"* HER *mother, whom* SHE *fears has been murdered in prison and her body parts "harvested" for the profit of wealthy and corrupt Chinese officials.*

(SUSAN *enters, carrying a jam box.* SHE *surveys the area, chooses a spot, sets box down, pushes play on* HER *box. We hear slow, calming, Chinese background music.* SUSAN *steps away from box, sets herself into the beginning position for exercise one in Falun Dafa: Buddha Showing a Thousand Hands.* SHE *sets* HER *feet about shoulder width apart, slightly bends* HER *knees, centers herself, closes* HER *eyes softly and breathes. Then* SHE *begins the movements, smoothly, unselfconsciously.* SHE *is obviously adept at the simple movements, having done them for years. After about twenty or thirty seconds,* MATT *enters quietly, watching* HER. HE *watches* HER *complete* HER *first set of movements. After* SHE *finishes,* SHE *opens* HER *eyes, and then looks at* HIM, *unselfconsciously.*)

SUSAN: Matt. You came here.

MATT: What are you doing?

SUSAN: Exercise. What are you doing?

MATT: I don't know. (SHE *turns off music.*) Are you in gymnastics?

SUSAN: When I was girl, in China, we do . . . gymnastics. This different. Falun Dafa. I do exercise here. Air clean; many trees; how well the living en . . . environment, here. Living environment well. Peace, here. (SHE *takes a deep breath, lets it out. Short silence.*)

MATT: Is your real name Susan?

SUSAN: Yes. My father American, you know; American—a—businessman in China. Marry Chinese woman, my mother.

MATT: That explains it. What is your Chinese name?

SUSAN: Susan.

MATT: No, your name in Chinese.

SUSAN: Dong Xue Tong.

MATT: Don . . . che . . .

SUSAN: Dong Xue Tong.

MATT: Are you a spy?

SUSAN: A spy?

MATT: Yeah.

SUSAN: How you spell?

MATT: S-p-y.

SUSAN: (*Sounding it out.*) Ssppyy—spy! No. Not spy. Why spy? You think I am spy?

MATT: No, I think you have a pretty smile.

(**SHE** *clearly doesn't understand this exchange.* **SHE** *looks puzzled, looks away, laughs a little.* **SHE** *turns back to* **HIM,** *not smiling.* **HE** *looks at* **HER,** *not knowing what to say. Then* **SHE** *smiles at* **HIM.** **HE** *smiles at* **HER.** **HER** *smile slowly fades.* **HIS** *also fades. Silence.*)

SUSAN: You stand, now. OK? Stand there. OK?

MATT: Yeah, I'm standing here.

(*Moves to* **HIM,** *stands next to* **HIM.** **SHE** *holds* **HER** *hands open to each other, and "rubs" them together with about an inch distance between them. Then* **SHE** *begins to slowly move* **HER** *hands along* **HIS** *back about an inch away from* **HIM,** *not touching* **HIM.**)

MATT: What are you doing?

SUSAN: Your energy . . . finding energy . . . flow. . . .

(*Then* **SHE** *moves* **HER** *hands down* **HIS** *back following the contours of* **HIS** *body.* **SHE** *goes all the way to* **HIS** *feet. Then* **SHE** *moves in front of* **HIM,** *moves* **HER** *hands down* **HIS** *arms, following the contours.* **SHE** *then begins at* **HIS** *navel, moves down* **HIS** *legs to* **HIS** *feet. Then* **SHE** *begins at the outside of both* **HIS** *shoulders and moves toward the center of* **HIS** *chest. Then* **SHE** *gets to* **HIS** *"heart."*)

SUSAN: Oh. . . .

MATT: What? (**SHE** *passes* **HER** *hands over* **HIS** *heart a number of times.*)

SUSAN: Energy . . . broken. (**HE** *steps away from* **HER**.)

MATT: What is that? What were you doing?

SUSAN: Finding your energy. I show you exercise?

MATT: What exercise?

SUSAN: This exercise help for energy. Energy blocked can flow again. Cleans energy and body. Then you not get sick. You want me to show . . . ? I still help you with algebra. (**HE** *hesitates.*) Your energy blocked, wrong color sometime. (*Again* **HE** *hesitates.*) Simple exercise. You see me tonight exercise. With Chinese music. (**SHE** *turns on Chinese music from before.*) Help you with your father. Your father. . . . (**SHE** *puts* **HER** *hand to* **HER** *heart.*)

MATT: My father? What about my father?

SUSAN: Exercise called "Buddha Showing a Thousand Hands." Heals energy.

MATT: What about my father?

SUSAN: Your father . . . you know.

MATT: What?

SUSAN: He . . . die.

MATT: How do you know my father died? How do you know these things about me?

SUSAN: I . . . read it.

MATT: Read it where?

Susan: I . . . read it.

Matt: Where?

Susan: I am not so good in Engrish and I—

Matt: You understand enough English to know what I'm asking you. You understand enough to read about my father. Where did you read it? (**She** *turns off music.*)

Susan: I am not so good in Engrish and I stay after school and study with teacher and she have . . . she have book on her desk. You write book.

Matt: You read my English journal?

Susan: Ju . . . jor . . . how you spell?

Matt: You read my journal for English class. No one was supposed to read that, not even the teacher. It says "Do Not Read" on the front.

Susan: Ms. Pritchard not know. You write about your father. He was sick long time. And then last summer, he die.

Matt: And that's why you've been watching me? Why you asked me to come here?

Susan: I understand.

Matt: Did your father die?

Susan: No, mother.

Matt: Your mother died?

Susan: Mother taken away, put in prison. By Chinese government.

Matt: That's different.

Susan: I don't know, alive, where is she? I don't know.

Matt: You don't know?

Susan: How can I know, alive or dead? I don't know.

Matt: What did your mother do? Why is she in prison?

Susan: Put in prison for living.

Matt: She must have done something.

Susan: She help people meet together. Like you and I; meet in park. Sometime talk. Sometime play music. Sometime read. Sometime exercise. That all. Just living. (*Silence.*) Like, police come and we arrested tonight; never see anyone again. For what?

Matt: You've been kind of stalking me. Watch me at school, reading my journal. Didn't you see "Do Not Read" on the cover?

Susan: Yes.

Matt: Then you shouldn't have read it. (**Susan** *goes to* **Him**, *puts* **Her** *arms around* **Him**. **He** *does not embrace* **Her** *back.*)

Susan: I will not . . . hurt you. (**She** *puts* **Her** *hands on* **His** *chest, slowly massages* **His** *"heart." Almost against* **His** *will this is soothing and surprisingly powerful for* **Him**.) I read your . . . heart in the book. I think: "This boy understand me. I want more to know him." (**He** *reaches up, takes* **Her** *hand, takes a deep breath.*) And today I see other students, angry at you. Leave you alone. You sit alone with music and . . . rock like child. And I think: "I understand this boy." (**He** *slowly breaks from* **Her**, *moves away.*)

Matt: Just because I came here tonight and said you had a pretty smile, that doesn't mean I want to date you. I'm sorry.

Susan: OK.

MATT: I . . . can't date anyone right now. You read my journal so you know everything that is going on.

SUSAN: OK. I not good date too.

MATT: Why?

SUSAN: I go away for long time.

MATT: When?

SUSAN: Maybe next—a—week. (*Short silence.*) I play Chinese music and show you exercise?

MATT: What exercise?

SUSAN: Falun Dafa.

MATT: How do you spell that?

SUSAN: F-a-l-u-n D-a-f-a.

MATT: Never heard of it.

SUSAN: Means: Great Law. Of life. Help heal energy.

MATT: (**HE** *considers.*) All right. (**SHE** *plays Chinese music.*)

SUSAN: Stand naturally. Feet like this; shoulders. Better standing stance. Relax body. Bend knees only little . . . (*Shoulder width apart.*) Hands . . . (**SHE** *shows* **HIM**.) Not touching. Slow, with music. Watch . . . stretch and relax, stretch and relax . . . (**SHE** *begins.* **HE** *tries to follow* **HER**. **SHE** *will instruct* **HIM** *with visual cues, such as raising* **HER** *elbows, or indicating that* **HER** *hands are not touching, that* **HER** *whole body is stretching, relaxing, etc.*) Stretch . . . relax . . . simplicity and ease . . . open, stretch . . . not think of anything . . . but moving . . . simplicity and ease . . . think of nothing but this . . . let energy move . . .

(**She** *smiles at* **Him** *when* **He** *follows* **Her** *well.* **They** *move through the first exercise completely. When* **They** *are finished,* **She** *turns off music.*)

Susan: How that? Better?

Matt: Yeah. (*To* **His** *surprise.*) Yeah! Better. Hot, I'm hot.

Susan: Opens all energy levels. Then you ab . . . absorb energy of universe. Make you hot.

Matt: Oh. Thanks.

Susan: Learn more next time. OK. Now you. Show American exercise.

Matt: American exercise? (**He** *thinks a moment.*) American exercise . . . (**He** *settles on one.* **He** *hands* **Her** *a CD,* **She** *puts it in player.*) Need music. Number three—is for exercise.

Susan: Number three; American Beethoven music. (**She** *plays music; a rock and roll song.*)

Matt: Turn it up. It's rock, baby. (**She** *turns it up.*) Listen to the music. Follow me. (**He** *starts doing jumping jacks.* **She** *follows.*) One-two. Three-four. One-two. Three-four. One-two. Three-four. (**He** *switches to windmills; touching the opposite hand to the foot.*) One-two-three-four. (**He** *switches to squat thrusts; squatting, putting hands on ground in front of* **Him**, *lunging back* **His** *legs till they're straight, then bringing them in again, and standing.*) One-two-three-four. (**She** *watches this, tries to do it.*) One-two-three-four. One-two-three-four. (*To the music,* **He** *exuberantly improvises* **His** *own exercise which is as close to a jumping dance as calisthenics.* **She** *tries to follow* **Him**. *Then* **He** *comes to some kind of end.* **He** *stops.*) The end. How's that? Better?

Susan: (*Over music.*) Better, I don't know. Why you do this?

MATT: Warm ups. Gets you moving, gets you rocking, gets you hot, gets you ready for anything.

SUSAN: I ready for anything.

MATT: You see? Gets you ready. (HE *impulsively kisses* HER *on the mouth, moves away.*)

SUSAN: I not ready there.

MATT: You got to be ready for anything. (*Pause, as* HE *continues to pound out the beat with* HIS *foot.*)

SUSAN: I ready now.

(HE *smiles at* HER. HE *continues improvising movements to the music.* SHE *begins to dance with* HIM, *improvising* HER *own movements, finding the rhythm of the song.* SHE *laughs. To this music,* HE *does rock versions of some of the movements from Buddha Showing a Thousand Hands.* SHE *sees this, and follows, laughs.* SHE *suddenly becomes sad, tears up, stops dancing, turns away from* HIM. HE *sees this, stops.* HE *sees* SHE's *clearly distressed.* HE *turns off music.*)

MATT: What's the matter?

SUSAN: My mother . . . I don't know . . . this is . . . fun; and . . . I like you . . . and I want to tell mother what we do. . . .

MATT: Yeah. My dad loved this music. Rocked on it all the time. He wanted us to play it at his funeral—and we did . . . and we tried to dance . . . I was dancing here, though, wasn't I? You got me dancing.

SUSAN: If I tell mother you play American music and exercise Falun Dafa, she angry—disrespect. Then I show her what you do and she laugh.

MATT: Sounds like I'd like her.

SUSAN: One day I come home from school and she gone. On birthday. My birthday they take her. Government call us evil; evil cult. Say we do mind control.

MATT: You, evil?

SUSAN: My mother teach me exercise; read to me Falun Gong. You think I am evil?

MATT: No.

SUSAN: How they know she Falun Gong, Matt?

MATT: I don't know.

SUSAN: I think . . . I am not sure . . . sister and I think: Yahoo.

MATT: Yahoo?

SUSAN: Yahoo tell government what she say on computer. Maybe that how they know.

MATT: Yahoo?

SUSAN: Yahoo say they do this. You see on Internet. Yahoo tell government names; government take many people we know. My sister Jane say government send mother to . . . re—edu . . . cation, labor camp. But, I don't know. Maybe mental hospital. Lock in mental hospital.

MATT: Is that true?

SUSAN: You look on Internet; find out. American people not—a— know much Falun Gong.

MATT: I never heard of it.

SUSAN: American people; American government not care. American companies make money in China. China big business for America.

Matt: Isn't your father an American businessman in China?

Susan: After government take—a—mother, government say we no longer live in China. Send us to America. Then company say father no longer work there.

Matt: They fired him?

Susan: China tell American company to do this. Tell America government not help father find mother. China money, big money, so America listen. What do I do, Matt?

Matt: I don't know.

Susan: I think and I think what do I do. My mother . . . many mother and father, need help. I read your book; you understand.

Matt: Yeah. I couldn't do anything.

Susan: You write that.

Matt: Nothing I could do but watch him get sicker, and thinner, and sicker.

Susan: You understand.

Matt: What can you do?

Susan: You know computer, Matt?

Matt: Computer? Yeah.

Susan: You know computer to . . . to . . . hack Yahoo?

Matt: You want to hack into Yahoo, on the computer?

Susan: I do it. I study computer in China, and I try and I try, but I cannot hack Yahoo. You show me.

Matt: I don't know how.

Susan: Who do know?

Matt: Quiz bowl boy might know.

Susan: Who?

Matt: Brandon. Karen's boyfriend.

Susan: You tell Brandon?

Matt: I can try, but . . . It's against the law. The police will arrest you; and maybe Brandon if he shows you.

Susan: I hack Yahoo, tell everyone what they do. Show picture of mother. Then it on American TV. On news. Falun Gong famous, then. Maybe America will help us.

Matt: You are a spy.

Susan: Not spy. Daughter. (*Silence.*) You tell Brandon?

SCENES FOR TWO WOMEN

AGNES OF GOD
BY JOHN PIELMEIER

In this scene, a novice nun gives birth to a baby, but when the infant is found suffocated in AGNES'*s convent room,* SHE *claims the child was the result of a "virgin birth." The* DOCTOR *in the scene, Martha, is a psychiatrist investigating the incident. Simply staged in a convent room with minimal furniture and props, the scene gradually intensifies to a point of maximum dramatic tension and character conflict at the very end, as modern science grapples with the paradox of a religious faith that verges on the pathological. The role of the* DOCTOR *can be played by a man or a woman.*

AGNES: Yes, Doctor?

DOCTOR: Agnes, I want you to tell me how you feel about babies.

AGNES: Oh, I don't like them. They frighten me. I'm afraid I'll drop them. They're always growing, you know. I'm afraid they'll grow too fast and wriggle right out of my arms. They have a soft spot on their heads and if you drop them they land on their heads and they become stupid. That's where I was dropped. You see, I don't understand things.

DOCTOR: Like what?

AGNES: Numbers. I don't understand where they're all headed. You could spend your whole life counting and never reach the end.

DOCTOR: I don't understand them either. Do you think I was dropped on my head?

AGNES: Oh, I hope not. It's a terrible thing, one of the great tragedies of life, to be dropped on your head. And there are other things, not just numbers.

DOCTOR: What things?

AGNES: Everything, sometimes. I wake up and I just can't get hold of the world. It won't stand still.

DOCTOR: So what do you do?

AGNES: I talk to God. He doesn't frighten me.

DOCTOR: Is that why you're a nun?

AGNES: I suppose so. I couldn't live without Him.

DOCTOR: But don't you think that God works through other religions, and other ways of life?

AGNES: I don't know.

DOCTOR: Couldn't I talk to Him?

AGNES: You could try. I don't know if He would listen to you.

DOCTOR: Why not?

AGNES: Because you don't listen to Him.

DOCTOR: Agnes, have you ever thought of leaving the convent? For something else?

AGNES: Oh no. There's nothing else. It makes me happy. Just being here helps me sleep at night.

DOCTOR: You have trouble sleeping?

AGNES: I get headaches. Mummy did too. She'd lie in the dark with a wet cloth over her face and tell me to go away. Oh, but she wasn't stupid. Oh no, she was very smart. She knew everything. She even knew things nobody else knew.

DOCTOR: What things?

AGNES: The future. She knew what was going to happen to me, and that's why she hid me away. I didn't mind that. I didn't like school very much. And I liked being with Mummy. She'd tell me all kinds of things. She told me I would enter the convent, and I did. She even knew about this.

DOCTOR: This?

AGNES: This.

DOCTOR: Me?

AGNES: This.

DOCTOR: How did she know . . . about this?

AGNES: Somebody told her.

DOCTOR: Who?

AGNES: I don't know.

DOCTOR: Agnes.

AGNES: You'll laugh.

DOCTOR: I promise I won't laugh. Who told her?

AGNES: An angel. When she was having one of her headaches. Before I was born.

DOCTOR: Did your mother see angels often?

AGNES: No. Only when she had her headaches. And not even then, sometimes.

DOCTOR: Do you see angels?

AGNES: (*A little too quickly.*) No.

DOCTOR: Do you believe that your mother really saw them?

AGNES: No. But I could never tell her that.

DOCTOR: Why not?

AGNES: She'd get angry. She'd punish me.

DOCTOR: How would she punish you?

AGNES: She'd . . . punish me.

DOCTOR: Did you love your mother?

AGNES: Oh, yes. Yes.

DOCTOR: Did you ever want to become a mother yourself?

AGNES: I could never be a mother.

DOCTOR: Why not?

AGNES: I don't think I'm old enough. Besides, I don't want a baby.

DOCTOR: Why not?

AGNES: Because I don't want one.

DOCTOR: But if you did want one, how would you go about getting one?

AGNES: I'd adopt it.

DOCTOR: Where would the adopted baby come from?

Agnes: From an agency.

Doctor: Before the agency.

Agnes: From someone who didn't want a baby.

Doctor: Like you?

Agnes: No! Not like me.

Doctor: But how would that person get the baby if they didn't want it?

Agnes: A mistake.

Doctor: How did your mother get you?

Agnes: A mistake! It was a mistake!

Doctor: Is that what she said?

Agnes: You're trying to get me to say that she was a bad woman, and that she hated me, and she didn't want me, but that is not true, because she did love me, and she was a good woman, a saint, and she did want me. You don't want to hear the nice parts about her—all you're interested in is sickness!

Doctor: Agnes, I cannot imagine that you know nothing about sex. . . .

Agnes: I can't help it if I'm stupid.

Doctor: . . . that you have no idea who the father of your child was. . . .

Agnes: They made it up!

Doctor: . . . that you have no remembrance of your impregnation. . . .

AGNES: It's not my fault!

DOCTOR: . . . and that you don't believe that you carried a child!

AGNES: It was a mistake!

DOCTOR: What, the child?

AGNES: Everything! Nuns don't have children!

DOCTOR: Agnes. . . .

AGNES: Don't touch me like that! Don't touch me like that! (**AGNES** *lashes out at the* **DOCTOR**, *who moves away*.) I know what you want from me! You want to take God away. You should be ashamed! They should lock you up. People like you!

REINCARNATION
BY JESSICA LITWAK

Belief in some version of life after death, including that of rein-carnation, surfaced in US society during the "new age" period of the 1970s and 1980s, and it is still widespread today. Here, the playwright combines this belief system with the popular notion of fortune-telling. What is normally a sacred point of belief in Hinduism and Buddhism inspires this hilarious scene in Litwak's piece, played out between a grizzled PSYCHIC *and a credulous, suicidal receptionist,* ROSIE, *who meet in a Manhattan storefront.*

ROSIE: How much?

PSYCHIC: Fifty.

ROSIE: Dollars?

PSYCHIC: Everybody charges. Ask.

ROSIE: Fifty dollars is an enormous amount of money.

PSYCHIC: Do or don't do. That's the price.

ROSIE: I have to think about expenses: rent, metro card, eggs, and—

PSYCHIC: Visa. MasterCard. No personal check.

ROSIE: . . . I just lost my job.

PSYCHIC: Madame Ceuili read hands, face, body hair. Fortune. Healing. Fix up de mess. God vil work miracle, Lady, but you got to meet him halfway. Forty-five dollar.

ROSIE: Forty-five?

PSYCHIC: I see everything.

ROSIE: Oh really? What color underpants am I wearing?

PSYCHIC: White. Embroidery says Saturday even though it's Tuesday afternoon.

ROSIE: Jesus.

PSYCHIC: Madame Ceuili can help you, Judith.

ROSIE: How did you . . . ?

PSYCHIC: Everything.

ROSIE: But I don't call myself Judith anymore. I go by my middle name, which is . . . ?

PSYCHIC: Whatever you want. I'm a busy woman.

ROSIE: I walk by here every day and you're always sitting in the window alone. (**MADAME CEUILI** *turns away.*) Can you tell me about my love life?

PSYCHIC: No problem, Lady.

ROSIE: And the possibility of future happiness?

PSYCHIC: Sure, sure. Love life. Happiness. Forty dollar. Last chance.

ROSIE: I hope I don't regret this. . . . (**ROSIE** *digs through* **HER** *purse and finds the money in small bills and coins.*)

Psychic: Hold the money in your hand and make a wish. (**Rosie** *closes* **Her** *eyes tight.* **Madame Ceuili** *grabs the money and stuffs it into* **Her** *bra.*) So. What did you wish for?

Rosie: Don't you know?

Psychic: Gonna get smart ass? (*Pause.*)

Rosie: Inner peace. And a boyfriend.

Psychic: Big wish. Need much assistance. Lemme see your hands. (**She** *grabs* **Rosie**'s *hands and turns them palms up.*) Oh God. Oh boy.

Rosie: What's wrong?

Psychic: Very bad. Head and heart line all mushed close together. CAUTION! WATCH OUT! Little lines here. Anxiety all around you. Confide in NO ONE! People talk behind your back. Natter natter. One lady wishes you very bad. Boss lady. Did you lose your job?

Rosie: I just told you I lost my job.

Psychic: Life line broken here. Bad luck. Accident in subway. Lots of smoke.

Rosie: WHAT?

Psychic: Let me see your eyes. Yep. Pig eyes. Like I thought. Bloodshot running all the way to center. Death in near future. Big accident.

Rosie: Oh God. When?

Psychic: Soon. Need to light a special emergency candle. Can you give up something so I can say important emergency prayer to discourage inevitable misfortune?

Rosie: Give up what?

Psychic: Both candle five dollar.

Rosie: I just gave you forty.

Psychic: Very bad accident. Bleeding from head. No one comes. Long death. Lying in pool of blood on subway floor, much old urine and chewing gum.

Rosie: OK. OK. (**Rosie** *scrambles around in* **Her** *purse for five dollars and hands it over.* **Madame Ceuili** *grabs the money and stuffs the money into* **Her** *bra.* **She** *lights a used candle.* **She** *picks up* **Rosie***'s palms, which are now shaking.*)

Psychic: Soft here under Mount of Venus. Pudgy. Like to please everybody. But fingers bend in toward middle, means nobody likes you back. Head line slopes down here. That's good. You speak wise words. But star on Mount of Jupiter means no one listens to anything you say. Let me see your eyebrows. Mmmmm. Thick. Dark. Hair grows all which way. Very bad luck with opposite sex. Mortal silk worm eyebrow, little dragon on the tail. You want to be popular but men don't like the way you smell. Lamb eyes. Live long life, but live it all alone.

Rosie: I thought you said I had pig eyes and was going to die on the subway.

Psychic: We fix that one with special candle. Now must take curse off heart line. Five more dollar for special candle.

Rosie: This is bullshit.

Psychic: Your aura is leaking. All color and energy pour out. Spirit seeping away. You spilling all over the place, Lady. You ain't never gonna fix nothin' even all the therapy you do. Seminar.

Workshop. Little happy sayings in mirror. Hitting pillow with baseball bat.

ROSIE: How did you—?

PSYCHIC: Madame Ceuili know everything. So. You want boyfriend or not? (ROSIE *counts out five dollars in change.* MADAME CEUILI *grabs the money and stuffs the money into* HER *bra.* MADAME CEUILI *lights another piece of candle.*) Let's see . . . lower lip bigger than top lip, means you want a husband with big arms. You got long rough hair. Not satisfied with first man so make wrong choice three times. Water shape body. Willow leaf in stream. Will marry late but family disown you. Some hair on chin. Marriage not successful unless husband homosexual.

ROSIE: COME ON!

PSYCHIC: Cow shape nose. You will have children but they will grow up to resent you and become incarcerated for drug-related crimes.

ROSIE: Bet you can fix all this for another five bucks.

PSYCHIC: Catching wind ears. Means unlucky with money.

ROSIE: That's for sure.

PSYCHIC: Poverty stricken. Unemployed. Nearly die of hunger at age fifty. Must light many candles to take away so many curses.

ROSIE: How many candles?

PSYCHIC: Very bad. Big mess. Many candles. At least five.

ROSIE: That's twenty-five dollars!

PSYCHIC: I'll make you a special deal. Eighteen dollars. Special price. You need it bad.

ROSIE: OK. That's it. This is ridiculous. I'm just gonna kill myself. (ROSIE *takes a noose, a razor, pills, and a large bottle of poison out of* HER *purse. As* SHE *does so,* MADAME CEUILI *protests.*)

PSYCHIC: Hey, hey wait. Lady. Hold on. Don't do nothing like that in my shop. Very bad. Big mess. Put back. Hey! I got something! Something else! An answer to your problems! (ROSIE *looks up.*) Reincarnation.

ROSIE: Reincarnation?

PSYCHIC: We gotta go back there. Take a look at your karma. It's the only way. This future business everyone wants to know. It sells big, but it don't teach nothing. Reincarnation is much better. Tells us about the Soul.

ROSIE: The soul?

PSYCHIC: It is ancient practice.

ROSIE: Have you ever tried it before?

PSYCHIC: You insult me, Lady. I am expert!

ROSIE: What do I have to do?

PSYCHIC: Very simple. Just return to the first Earth life relevant to the one today and repeat the life cycle backwards experiencing as many incarnations as possible. Cross repeatedly back and forth the chasm that separates birth and death to find your source.

ROSIE: OY.

PSYCHIC: Your subconscious mind contains all memories of previous life. Human brains are like anchors that have lain too long on the ocean floor. They must be lifted out of muddy deception. We must ATTAIN THE ILLUMINATION. We must SEARCH

FOR THE GOLD. I will guide you on this journey by transferring my wisdom to your body with special techniques.

Rosie: Like a mind meld?

Psychic: This is not science fiction, Lady. This is Supreme Truth! Do or don't do. I could care less.

Rosie: Does it hurt?

Psychic: Every lifetime hurts a little bit. Some more than others.

Rosie: Well . . . I have nowhere else to go this afternoon.

Psychic: OK. REINCARNATION PACKAGE DELUXE. (**Rosie** *puts* **Her** *suicide tools away with newfound hope*.)

Rosie: Reincarnation Package Deluxe!

Psychic: Five lifetimes for one hundred.

Rosie: Dollars?

Psychic: Very draining. Much psychic energy. Extremely delicate work. To bring you back in one piece.

Rosie: I gave you everything I had for my phone bill and a new bra. I lost my job. There's a recession. What am I supposed to do? (**She** *looks in* **Her** *bag*.)

Psychic: OK. OK. Listen. You in big trouble. Life falling down. I make you a deal. Mini deluxe. Three lifetimes for twenty-five dollars. And your eyeglasses.

Rosie: Why do you want my glasses?

Psychic: To read! *People* magazine. The Bible. All them letters are so teeny weeny . . . can't see a fucking thing.

Rosie: I can't see without my glasses.

Psychic: Maybe you see better after past life regression. Clean up your karma, clear up your sight. Do or don't do. I could care less.

Rosie: I must be nuts. (**Rosie** *hands over* **Her** *glasses and then fumbles blindly in* **Her** *purse for* **Her** *wallet. The* **Psychic** *takes money out for* **Her** *and shoves bills into* **Her** *bra. The* **Psychic** *lifts* **Her** *crystal ball.*)

Psychic: Focus on the crystal. Never take your eyes off it. Keep your eyes open. Keep your feet on the floor! (**She** *puts the crystal in front of* **Rosie**. **She** *closes* **Her** *eyes. Swaying back and forth.* **Rosie** *fidgets, crosses* **Her** *legs.*) FEET ON THE FLOOR! (**Rosie** *looks around the room.*) EYES ON THE CRYSTAL! (**Rosie** *stares at the crystal. Strange music. Lights flicker.*) Time is flowing backward. See the road of living memory flowing from the center of self to the deepest heart of the crystal. A thin blue patch of mist. Concentrate! (*Smoke. Lights shift.* **Rosie**'s *body sways and moves, contorting into a different being. The* **Psychic** *claps. Lights brighten suddenly and* **Rosie** *is someone else.*) Nineteen hundred and two. Where are you? Look around.

Rosie: (*In a thick Irish brogue.*) Small room. Window with bars. Steel. Dusty glass. I been here a long time. No one to talk to.

Psychic: What's your name?

Rosie: Mary.

Psychic: Mary. (*Suddenly* **Rosie/Mary** *snaps* **Her** *head around and* **Her** *tone changes.* **She** *speaks with a thick Irish brogue.*)

Rosie: Oh, come on, Nursey, don't just shove it under the door and go off. Come on and sit a bloody minute? Everybody keeps so far off. I hear 'em whisperin' as they run past. Staring in at me like a circus freak. Why doesn't anyone like me, Nursey? Wait! Don't go. Listen, could you bring us a hot plate with a fry pan, maybe a small wooden spoon, a mixin' bowl? I need my tools of the trade.

Psychic: You're a cook?

Rosie: I'm a good cook. Oh! Nursey let me cook for you. I'll make ya something grand. I learned my trade on the ship comin' to America. Typhoid fever killed everyone on board 'cept fer me and the cook. He taught me how ta spice meat. Then I worked in a fancy hotel in New York. When four of the cooks took sick they promoted me from apprentice and gave me a chance at me very own soup. That was how I got my start. When all them cooks died plus a waiter they went and shut that place down and I got me a job in private house. Mrs. Delbert Scott. She loved oxtail soup.

Psychic: Oxtail soup? (*As* **Rosie/Mary** *talks,* **She** *mimes the gestures of cooking: tearing meat, etc. with* **Her** *hands.* **She** *also repeatedly wipes* **Her** *nose and sneezes into* **Her** *hands.*)

Rosie: Oxtail soup. Ya cut up an oxtail wit a choppin' knife, rub him with lard and braise him in a fry pan 'til he turns brown, then add two pound of cabbage and nine medium onions and boil for two hours. Then tear the meat into small tiny pieces wit yar hands and throw 'em back into the broth. Simmer one hour, serve hot.

Psychic: Sounds . . . tasty . . .

Rosie: Mrs. Delbert got sick and died after my third week. After that I went to Mr. Newton on East Sixteenth Street. He loved rice pudding. He got real sick after I'd been with him for only a short while. I nursed him 'til his death with utmost care. That summer there were three thousand four hundred sixty-seven cases of typhoid in New York. The coppers grabbed me at the green grocers. I was buyin' carrots for a beef stew. They wrapped me in a blanket and dragged me in here. Locked all the doors. Now people treat me as a monster. Shove little trays under me door. Not good food neither, but stale breads and inferior broths. I don't have me own kitchen. I can't bake, fry, or chop. What kind of life is this? I might as well kill meself. (*The* **PSYCHIC** *grabs the crystal, holds it up and makes strange keening noises. The lights flicker and* **ROSIE** *comes back to herself.*) TYPHOID MARY? I WAS TYPHOID MARY.

PSYCHIC: Hold on for number two!

ROSIE: Wait. . . . (*The* **PSYCHIC** *holds the crystal. Smoke. Lights shift.* **ROSIE**'s *body sways and contorts. The* **PSYCHIC** *claps. Lights brighten.* **ROSIE** *is someone else.* **SHE** *speaks as a young girl with a cockney accent.*)

PSYCHIC: Hundred and sixty-four. Where are you?

ROSIE: Dark place. Spiders.

PSYCHIC: What are you doing there?

ROSIE: Waiting to burn.

PSYCHIC: Your name?

ROSIE: Agnes, Mum. Agnes Duncan.

PSYCHIC: Are you a witch, Agnes?

ROSIE: They tell me so, Mum. And it must be, all the evidence against me. Can a person be a witch without knowing it?

PSYCHIC: I doubt it, Agnes.

ROSIE: I'm evil.

PSYCHIC: Evil?

ROSIE: All women is evil, Mum. "She is given to avarice and superstition. She is an inescapable punishment, a temptation, a calamity, a domestic danger. Her voice is false, she is a liar by nature. She follows her impulse without sense, has a weak memory, a slippery tongue, and an insatiable carnal lust which is the root of all witchcraft." Judge told me to memorize all the facts of women's sins before I die so as to save my soul. We incline the minds of men to passion and then remove the members accommodated to that act, change 'em into beasts, seduce virgins, devour children, cause famine, transport ourselves through air on broomsticks, and have weird lurid parties where we take turns kissing the devil's bum.

PSYCHIC: Have you done these things, Agnes?

ROSIE: They tell me so, Mum. But in truth I don't remember them.

PSYCHIC: How old are you?

ROSIE: Fourteen years.

PSYCHIC: What else did the Judge tell you?

ROSIE: Told me my three-legged dog was a familiar to me.

PSYCHIC: What did you say?

ROSIE: I said course she's familiar. I had her since she was a pup and got runned down by horses. They said she was a demon and must suckle at my witches tit here on the leg . . . thing I'd always taken for a birth mole. Glynnis Baines said she heard my dog talking to me in the woods, said I called it Satan. Said she heard me call out "Come here, Satan." But the dog is Sadie, Mum. I called out "Come here Sadie." They took her away and shaved off her fur and burned her up. I cried terrible then but they said the tears of witches is false tears made up of the blood of angels.

Psychic: I don't think you are a witch, Agnes.

Rosie: They said my hair is long and shiny and the Devil always picks girls with beautiful hair.

Psychic: You are not a witch.

Rosie: A man from our village swore he's seen me raise a storm by taking my stockings off. The Judge piled up all the evidence against me like rocks. So I confessed.

Psychic: You confessed?

Rosie: They tortured me cruel then, Mum, with the thumbscrew and the rack and wheel. They took off me clothes and shaved the hair on my privacies and whipped me down there. And finally on the fourth day I marked X on a paper by my name Agnes to make them stop. And they said it was my confession and I was to die. And I'll burn next Saturday on Castle Hill. They say to drink no water for three days before. The drier you are the faster you burn. I do pray, Mum. I want to face death bravely in the eye, but truth is . . . I'm scared. (*The* **Psychic** *grabs the crystal, holds it up, and makes strange keening noises. The lights flicker and* **Rosie** *comes back to herself.*) I WAS BURNED AS A WITCH? WHY ME?

Psychic: There were nine million women burned as witches in Europe in the fourteenth and fifteenth centuries. So by my calculations there are probably quite a few burned witches walking around Manhattan. Not to mention New Jersey—

Rosie: Jesus! I've been whining for four hundred years!

Psychic: It's your karma, Lady.

Rosie: My karma?

Psychic: Cause and effect. Do bad thing in one life, suffer in the next.

Rosie: What could I have done that was so horrible?

Psychic: Ready for lifetime number three?

Rosie: NO! (*The* **Psychic** *holds the crystal. Lights shift.* **Rosie** *contorts. The* **Psychic** *claps. Lights brighten.* **Rosie** *is someone else.*)

Psychic: Twelve hundred and forty-five BC.

Rosie: My beautiful children! My sweet babes, my dearest darlings. I who nursed you at my breast and swaddled your soft bodies in warm cloth. I who rocked you to sleep with soft music in the dead of night. I who taught you speech and prayer. I who gave you birth must now slash your little throats with my great big sword and rip the life from your little bodies. For your father, who I nurtured though hard times and offered up my arts and herbs to find his bloody golden fleece and gave up all my best unsaggy years to suit his pleasure, has betrayed me to a blond bitch and made her his legal wife before Colchis and the Gods. And he will suffer deep and ever feel regret when he beholds your lifeless forms and knows that I have MURDERED YOU! BRING ME ROPES TO BIND MY LITTLE CHILDREN! BRING ME MY GREAT BIG SWORD! GODDESSES HAVE MERCY ON ME. OF ALL THINGS UPON EARTH THAT BLEED AND GROW, THE HERB MOST BRUISED IS WOMAN! I AM HAVING A REALLY BAD DAY! (**Rosie** *squirms, trying to fight* **Her** *way out of Medea.*) Help . . . help! (*The* **Psychic** *grabs the crystal. The lights flicker and* **Rosie** *comes back to herself.*) Typhoid Mary, burned as a witch, and Medea. I must have the worst karma in history.

Psychic: It ranks right up there.

Rosie: Why couldn't I have been a role model like Amelia Earhart?

Psychic: You weren't her.

Rosie: How do you know?

Psychic: Timing is off. You were Typhoid Mary until 1938. Anyway your three lives are up. Have a nice day. Please come again.

Rosie: Wait!

Psychic: Sorry Lady. Time is up. Gotta go now.

Rosie: I feel worse than when I came in here. I—

Psychic: Bye, bye!

Rosie: I want my money back!

Psychic: Don't be crazy.

Rosie: GIVE ME MY MONEY BACK!!! (**Rosie** *dives at the* **Psychic** *and shoves* **Her** *hands down the woman's bra where* **She** *has seen all of* **Her** *money disappear.* **They** *struggle. The* **Psychic**'s *turban is knocked off.*)

Psychic: (*In a thick Brooklyn accent.*) WHAT THE FUCK YOU THINK YOU'RE DOIN'? (**Rosie** *stares at* **Her.**)

Rosie: What did you say?

Psychic: Get your fucking hands off me.

Rosie: Where is your Romanian accent? (*Pause.*)

Psychic: Shit.

Rosie: You're a phony.

Psychic: Damn.

Rosie: I knew this was a scam. What's your name—not Madame thingamajig. . . . (*Long pause.*) WELL?

Psychic: Dorothy. Dorothy Gennelli.

Rosie: Where are you from, Dorothy? Not Romania!

Dorothy: Brooklyn.

Rosie: It's a criminal offense tricking people. I'm gonna report you!

Dorothy: To who?

Rosie: The . . . the Better Business Bureau. The psychic police.

Dorothy: Look, I did the three lives. Now get out.

Rosie: You should be ashamed of yourself.

Dorothy: Don't lecture me. Everybody has to make a living.

Rosie: This is your career choice? Phony fortune teller?

Dorothy: Lady, I got three kids. Eleven, eight, and five. When my husband left I had no marketable skills.

Rosie: I got no marketable skills either. But I'm not a liar or a cheat. I'm a secretary! Or at least I was before lunch.

Dorothy: I tried secretarial work but my spirit felt constrained in those small cubicles. I also tried waitressing but the hours were so bad. Mostly evenings. My youngest, Sally, can't fall asleep unless I lay down beside her and stroke her hair.

Rosie: So you decided to become clairvoyant?

Dorothy: I've always been sensitive to the supernatural. Ever since I was a little girl. I heard voices.

Rosie: Now you're Joan of Arc?

Dorothy: Not saints, dead people. I'd look at someone and suddenly I'd hear the voices of all the people they had been before. Queens, Kings, Prostitutes, Spies. I couldn't control it. My parents used to lock me up in my room during dinner parties so I wouldn't blurt out the embarrassing past life of one of their guests. They thought I was crazy. Spouting lies. So my Dad sent me to convent school.

Rosie: I don't need to hear your whole life story.

Dorothy: And the nuns beat the voices out of my head.

Rosie: You stole my money, you fake.

Dorothy: I am not a fake. Not completely. I see the past. I can send people back. I sent you back. That was real, wasn't it?

Rosie: What about the future?

Dorothy: I studied hard. Late nights when the kids were asleep. Chinese face-reading. Ancient Egyptian palms.

Rosie: The Gypsy dialect, too, that must have been time consuming.

Dorothy: All this stuff—the voice, the costume—people need that to believe. But I'm not a con artist, Rosie. I take past life regression very seriously. I have a gift for it.

Rosie: Yeah, you have a gift. Historical torture.

Dorothy: Do you know what it's like taking your kids to school every morning and waving goodbye with all the nice normal parents and then rushing into the bathroom of a coffee shop to transform yourself into a gypsy with a hairy mole?

Rosie: That's not a real mole?

DOROTHY: Just so you can sit in a storefront window, trying to look exotic enough to get someone, anyone, to come through that door.

ROSIE: Like a suicidal receptionist?

DOROTHY: You are my first customer in three days.

ROSIE: I'm supposed to feel sorry for you?

DOROTHY: I hide my job from my kids so they won't be embarrassed. Can you imagine if one of their teachers saw me like this? Angela is just developing breasts. Appearance is everything to her. She'd just die if she knew how I pay the bills. And I can barely pay 'em. Your eyeglasses are for Theresa, my middle girl. She can hardly see the chalkboard or the TV across the room. I got no health insurance. How am I gonna pay for glasses? I hope your prescription fits her. I just can't make ends meet no more. There's a man in Queens, Joey Amalia. He wants to marry me. He is not an attractive man, and I wouldn't call him friendly. But he owns his own deli, which has very good salami and Italian cheese—

ROSIE: This is extremely depressing. I am sorry that you have so many personal problems, but I'm in real mess here. You were my last stab at self-esteem. Now I find out I've been a murderess, a witch, and a typhoid carrier. I have been miserable for over two thousand years. (*Silence. Suddenly* **ROSIE** *gets an idea.* **SHE** *looks at* **DOROTHY**.) I can't do this anymore.

DOROTHY: Please don't pull out all your equipment. I can't handle it.

ROSIE: Every summer my mom sent me to Girl Scout camp on the Wanhee-Wanhee River. The summer I was ten they promised each of us girls a baby chicken. We could hardly wait. It was during canoe lessons when we finally saw this lady coming over the hill with a box. There were cheeping noises coming from the box. And the counselor, I think it was Big Betty, called us over. There were twenty-three of us. We all ran over and stuck our heads into the box and there were twenty-two fluffy yellow chickens cheeping and jumping around. And then I saw this one chicken lying face down on the bottom of the box. And I looked up at Big Betty and I said, "My little chicken is dead."

Dorothy: Oh God.

Rosie: I am sick of having a dead chicken.

Dorothy: What?

Rosie: MY CHICKEN IS ALIVE!

Dorothy: Calm down.

Rosie: DO IT AGAIN.

Dorothy: What?

Rosie: LOOK AGAIN. FOR SOMEONE HEROIC!

Dorothy: I looked.

Rosie: At three lousy lifetimes. There must be other ones. How many lives does a person get?

Dorothy: It depends. Could be hundreds.

Rosie: Look again.

Dorothy: Not just people either. You could have been a dog. Or a chicken. (**Rosie** *hands* **Dorothy** *the crystal ball.* **Dorothy** *dodges, refusing to touch it.*)

Rosie: There's gotta be somebody somewhere when I did something brave.

Dorothy: (*Overlapping.*) It's late, I gotta get going.

Rosie: (*Overlapping.*): I gotta get my money's worth.

Dorothy: (*Overlapping.*) It's a long walk to the F train.

Rosie: (*Overlapping.*) It won't take that long. One more lifetime!

Dorothy: I'm a phony, you said it yourself.

Rosie: I didn't mean it. You're gifted. You have a gift. I got no gifts. You gotta help me find something good.

Dorothy: Come back tomorrow.

Rosie: I can't wait until tomorrow, I have to do this now. There is somebody better back there. I know there is.

Dorothy: I can't guarantee that. Things might be even worse. I have no control over your past. Karma is karma.

Rosie: I AM CHANGING MY FUCKING KARMA! (**Rosie** *shoves the crystal ball into* **Dorothy**'s *hands. Smoke. Lights shift.* **Dorothy**'s *body contorts. Lights brighten.* **Dorothy** *is someone else, an old* **Black Woman** [**Sylvie**] *with a big deep voice.*)

Dorothy: (*As* **Sylvie**.) My Master hardly never beat me none but that wife of his she whopped me eve'y chance. She'd level me with wood, tong, knife, ax, anything that was handiest and she was damn quick about it too.

Rosie: Eighteen hundred and sixty-two.

Dorothy: (*As* **Sylvie**.) One day I was in the dining room. She wanted things to look stylish. I didn't do it to suit her, she scolded me and I sassed her, and she struck me with the fire shovel and broke my head. I set down my tools then and I squared for a fight. First whack I struck her a hell of a blow with my fist. I didn't knock her entirely through the panels of the wall but her landing made a terrible smash and I didn't know myself but that I'd killed the old devil. My massa called fo me then and I thought he was gonna beat me hard, but he say "Sylvie you and your mistress get along so badly, if you go up North and you stay there, I will give you free." And he wrote me out a pass and early the next morning I set out. But I didn't go north. I crossed over the river and headed down to Georgia to find my mama to purchase her up outta bondage. But you child . . . (**She** *grabs* **Rosie**'s *arms*.) . . . You get to grow up free. So don't you never let nobody beat you, daughter. You stand up tall. And you square your fist! (**Rosie** *sets the crystal down. The lights flicker,* **Dorothy** *comes back to herself.*)

Rosie: Wow. You were incredible.

Dorothy: Do you realize what you just did?

Rosie: What?

Dorothy: You sent me back. You did.

Rosie: I just picked up the crystal thingie—

Dorothy: You set the karmic energies in motion. No one can regress without a push. You shifted time. And you brought back someone strong and heroic. You do have a gift, Rosie. You can do this.

Rosie: Do what? Reincarnation?

Dorothy: You should go into this line of work. Help people. It's certainly one way to burn off all that karma of yours.

Rosie: But I need to go back there myself, find someone courageous.

Dorothy: You can only be brave in present tense.

ROSIE: How do I—

DOROTHY: Practice. (**DOROTHY** *places* **HER** *turban on* **ROSIE***'s head. Blackout. End of play.*)

MARISOL
BY JOSÉ RIVERA

Marisol is asleep on Her bed with Her eyes shut throughout this nightmare scene, although She responds to the Angel almost consciously, as the stage directions indicate. At this point in the play, Marisol is desperately struggling to reconcile Her religious beliefs with the suffering and depravity that She encounters in Her everyday life in the Bronx. The scene is structured very carefully, rising through a series of smaller conflicts and becoming more intense for both characters, until it reaches a powerful climax at the very end. Rivera's apocalyptic vision of the end of modern society in this play raises many questions about how religion has become a social convention, how greed can coexist with a deeply felt need for social justice, and why existential angst is so prevalent in our modern world.

ANGEL: A man is worshipping a fire hydrant on Taylor Avenue, Marisol. He's draping rosaries on it, genuflecting hard. An old woman's selling charmed chicken blood in see-through zip-lock bags for a buck. They're setting another homeless man on fire in Van Cortland Park. (*The ANGEL rattles the metal gate.*) Cut that shit out, you fucking Nazis! (*The ANGEL goes to MARISOL's door and checks the locks. SHE stomps cockroaches. SHE straightens up a little.*) I swear, best thing that could happen to this city is immediate evacuation followed by fire on a massive scale. Melt it all down. Consume the ruins. Then put the ashes of those evaporated dreams into a big urn and sit the urn on the desks of a few thousand oily politicians. Let them smell the disaster like we do. (*The* ANGEL *goes to* MARISOL's *bed and looks at* HER. MARISOL's *heart beats faster as* SHE *starts to hyperventilate.*) So what do you believe in, Marisol? You believe in me? Or do you believe your senses? If so, what's that taste in your mouth? (*The* ANGEL *clicks* HER *fingers.*)

MARISOL: (*In* HER *sleep, tasting.*) Oh my God, arroz con gandules! Yum!

ANGEL: What's your favorite smell? (*Click.*)

MARISOL: (*In* HER *sleep, sniffing.*) The ocean! I smell the ocean!

ANGEL: Do you like sex?

(*Click!* MARISOL *is seized by powerful sexual spasms that wrack* HER *body and nearly throw* HER *off the bed. When they end,* MARISOL *stretches out luxuriously: exhausted but happy.*)

MARISOL: (*Laughing.*) I've got this wild energy running through my body! (*The* ANGEL *gets closer to* HER.)

ANGEL: Here's your big chance, baby. What would you like to ask the Angel of the Lord?

MARISOL: (*In* HER *sleep, energized.*) Are you real? Are you true? Are you gonna make the Bronx safe for me? Are you gonna make miracles and reduce my rent? Is it true angels' favorite food is Thousand Island dressing? Is it true your shit smells like mangos and when you're drunk you speak Portuguese?! (*The* ANGEL *laughs.*)

ANGEL: Honey, last time I was drunk. . . .

MARISOL: (*A horrifying realization.*) Wait a minute—am I dead? Did I die tonight? How did I miss that? Was it the man with the golf club? Did he beat me to death? Oh my God. I've been dead all night. And when I look around I see that Death is my ugly apartment in the Bronx. No this can't be Death! Death can't have this kind of furniture!

ANGEL: God you're so cute, I could eat you up. No. You're still alive.

(MARISOL *is momentarily relieved—then* SHE *suddenly starts touching* HER *stomach as* SHE *gets a wild, exhilarating idea.*)

MARISOL: (*In* HER *sleep.*) Am I pregnant with the Lord's baby?! Is the new Messiah swimming in my electrified womb? Is the supersperm of God growing a mythic flower deep in the secret greenhouse inside me? Will my morning sickness taste like communion wine? This is amazing—billions of women on earth, and I get knocked up by God!

ANGEL: No baby, no baby, no baby, no baby—No. Baby. (*Beat.* MARISOL *is a little disappointed.*)

MARISOL: (*In* HER *sleep.*) No? Then what is it? Are you real or not? 'Cause if you're real and God is real and the Gospels are real, this would be the perfect time to tell me. 'Cause I once looked for angels, I did, in every shadow of my childhood—but I never found any. I thought I'd find you hiding inside the notes I sang to myself as a kid. The songs that helped me to sleep and kept me from killing myself with fear. But I didn't see you then. (*The* ANGEL *doesn't answer.* HER *silence—*HER *very presence—starts to unhinge* MARISOL.) C'mon! Somebody up there has to tell me why I live the way I do! What's going on here anyway? Why is there a war on children in this city? Why are apples extinct? Why are they planning to drop human insecticide on overpopulated areas of the Bronx? Why has the color blue disappeared from the sky? Why does common rainwater turn your skin bright red? Why do cows give salty milk? Why did the Plague kill half my friends? AND WHAT HAPPENED TO THE MOON? Where did the moon go? How come nobody's seen it in nearly nine months . . . ?

(**MARISOL** *is trying desperately to keep from crying. The* **ANGEL** *gets into bed with* **MARISOL**. *Contact with the* **ANGEL** *makes* **MARISOL** *gasp.* **SHE** *opens* **HER** *mouth to scream, but nothing comes out.* **MARISOL** *collapses—***HER** *whole body goes limp.* **MARISOL** *rests* **HER** *head on the* **ANGEL**'*s lap. Electricity surges gently through* **MARISOL**'*s body.* **SHE** *is feeling no pain, fear, or loneliness. The* **ANGEL** *strokes* **HER** *hair.*)

ANGEL: I kick-started your heart, Marisol. I wired your nervous system. I pushed your fetal blood in the right direction and turned the foam in your infant lungs to oxygen. When you were six and your parents were fighting, I helped you pretend you were underwater: that you were a cold-blooded fish, in the bottom of the black ocean, far away and safe. When racist motherfuckers ran you out of school at ten screaming. . . .

MARISOL: (*In* **HER** *sleep.*) . . . "kill the spik . . . ."

ANGEL: I turned the monsters into little columns of salt! At last count, one plane crash, one collapsed elevator, one massacre at the hands of a right-wing fanatic with an Uzi, and sixty-six thousand six hundred and three separate sexual assaults never happened because of me.

MARISOL: (*In* **HER** *sleep.*) Wow. Now I don't have to be so paranoid . . . ? (*The* **ANGEL** *suddenly gets out of bed.* **MARISOL** *curls up in a fetal position. The* **ANGEL** *is nervous now, full of hostile energy: anxious.*)

ANGEL: Now the bad news. (*The* **ANGEL** *goes to the window.* **SHE**'*s silent a moment as* **SHE** *contemplates the devastated Bronx landscape.*

The ANGEL *finds it very hard to tell* MARISOL *what's on* HER *mind.*)

MARISOL: (*In* HER *sleep, worried.*) What?

ANGEL: I can't expect you to understand the political ins and outs of what's going on. But you have eyes. You asked me questions about children and water and war and the moon: the same questions I've been asking myself for a thousand years. (*We hear distant explosions.* MARISOL's *body responds with a jolt.*)

MARISOL: (*In* HER *sleep, quiet.*) What's that noise?

ANGEL: The universal body is sick, Marisol. Constellations are wasting away, the nauseous stars are full of blisters and sores, the infected earth is running a temperature, and everywhere the universal mind is wracked with amnesia, boredom, and neurotic obsessions.

MARISOL: (*In* HER *sleep, frightened.*) Why?

ANGEL: Because God is old and dying and taking the rest of us with Him. And for too long, much too long, I've been looking the other way. Trying to stop the massive hemorrhage with my little hands. With my prayers. Believing if I could only love God more, things would get better. But it didn't work and I knew if I didn't do something soon, it would be too late.

MARISOL: (*In* HER *sleep, frightened.*) What did you do?

ANGEL: I called a meeting. And I urged the Heavenly Hierarchies— the Seraphim, Cherubim, Thrones, Dominions, Principalities, Powers, Virtues, Archangels, and Angels—to vote to stop the universal ruin . . . by slaughtering our senile God. And they did. Listen well, Marisol: angels are going to kill the King of Heaven and restore the vitality of the universe with His blood.

And I'm going to lead them. (**Marisol** *takes this in silently— then suddenly erupts—***Her** *body shaking with fear and energy.*)

Marisol: (*In* **Her** *sleep.*) Okay, I wanna wake up now!

Angel: There's going to be a war.

Marisol: (*In* **Her** *sleep.*) GOD IS GREAT! GOD IS GOOD! THANK YOU FOR OUR NEIGHBORHOOD!

Angel: Soon we're going to send out spies, draft able-bodied celestial beings, raise taxes. . . .

Marisol: (*In* **Her** *sleep.*) THANK YOU FOR THE BIRDS THAT SING! THANK YOU GOD FOR EVERYTHING!

Angel: Soon we're going to take off our wings of peace, Marisol, and put on our wings of war. Then we're going to spread blood and vigor across the sky and reawaken the dwindling stars!

Marisol: (*In* **Her** *sleep, reciting fast.*) "And there was war in Heaven; Michael and his angels fought against the dragon; and the dragon fought—"

Angel: It could be suicide. A massacre. He's better armed. Better organized. And, well, a little omniscient. But we have to win. (*Beat.*) And when we do win . . . when we crown the new God and begin the new millennium, sister . . . the earth will be restored. The moon will return. The degradation of the animal kingdom will end. Men and women will be elevated to a higher order. All children will speak Latin. And Creation will finally be perfect. (*Distant thunder and lightning. The* **Angel** *quickly goes to the window to read the message in the lightning.* **She** *turns to* **Marisol**, *who is struggling to wake up.*) It also means I have to leave you. I can't stay. I can't protect you anymore. (*Beat.*)

Marisol: (*In **Her** sleep.*) What? You're leaving me? I'm gonna be alone?

Angel: I don't want to. I love you. I thought you had to know. But now I have to go and fight. And so do you.

Marisol: (*In **Her** sleep, terrified.*) I don't know how to fight!

Angel: You can't endure anymore. You can't trust luck or prayer or mercy or other people. When I drop my wings, all hell's going to break loose and soon you're not going to recognize the world—so get yourself some power, Marisol, whatever you do.

Marisol: (*In **Her** sleep.*) What's gonna happen to me without you . . . ? (*The **Angel** goes to **Marisol** and tries to kiss **Her**.*)

Angel: I don't know. (**Marisol** *lashes out, trying to hit the* **Angel**. **Marisol** *spits at the* **Angel**. *The* **Angel** *grabs* **Marisol**'s *hands.*)

Marisol: I'm gonna be meat! I'M GONNA BE FOOD!! (*The* **Angel** *holds the struggling* **Marisol**.)

Angel: Unless you want to join us. . . .

Marisol: NOOOOOOOO!!

DOUBT: A PARABLE
BY JOHN PATRICK SHANLEY

The ever-present tension between doubt, obedience, and faith is the focus of this Pulitzer-winning drama. In the following scene, the young SISTER JAMES *struggles unsuccessfully to resist the authority of* HER *older mentor and role model,* SISTER ALOYSIUS, *who suspects* THEIR *parish priest is a sexual predator. The drama never answers this question with any certitude, and hence explores the tangled human emotions of suspicion, trust, envy, and self-honesty against the backdrop of clerical celibacy in the Roman Catholic Church. There are many discoveries for each of the actors to play in the scene, which takes place as* THEY *are gardening.* THEIR *conflict builds to a sharp climax at the end as* SISTER JAMES *uses the children in the playground as an excuse to get away from the suspicions and questions of* SISTER ALOYSIUS.

SISTER JAMES: The Monsignor is very good, isn't he?

SISTER ALOYSIUS: Yes. But he is oblivious.

SISTER JAMES: To what?

SISTER ALOYSIUS: I don't believe he knows who's President of the United States. I mean him no disrespect of course. It's just that he's otherworldly in the extreme.

SISTER JAMES: Is it that he's innocent, Sister Aloysius?

SISTER ALOYSIUS: You have a slyness at work, Sister James. Be careful of it. How is your class? How is Donald Muller?

SISTER JAMES: He is thirteenth in class.

SISTER ALOYSIUS: I know. That's sufficient. Is he being accepted?

SISTER JAMES: He has no friends.

SISTER ALOYSIUS: That would be a lot to expect after only two months. Has anyone hit him?

SISTER JAMES: No.

SISTER ALOYSIUS: Someone will. And when it happens, send them right down to me.

SISTER JAMES: I'm not so sure anyone will.

SISTER ALOYSIUS: There is a statue of St. Patrick on one side of the church altar and a statue of St. Anthony on the other. This parish serves Irish and Italian families. Someone will hit Donald Muller.

SISTER JAMES: He has a protector.

SISTER ALOYSIUS: Who?

SISTER JAMES: Father Flynn. (**SISTER ALOYSIUS**, *who has been fussing with mulch, is suddenly rigid.* **SHE** *rises.*)

SISTER ALOYSIUS: What?

SISTER JAMES: He's taken an interest. Since Donald went on altar boys. (*Pause.*) I thought I should tell you.

SISTER ALOYSIUS: I told you to come to me, but I hoped you never would.

SISTER JAMES: Maybe I shouldn't have.

SISTER ALOYSIUS: I knew once you did, something would be set in motion. So it's happened.

SISTER JAMES: What?! I'm not telling you that! I'm not even certain what you mean.

SISTER ALOYSIUS: Yes, you are.

SISTER JAMES: I've been trying to become more cold in my thinking, as you suggested . . . I feel as if I've lost my way a little, Sister Aloysius. I had the most terrible dream last night. I want to be guided by you and responsible to the children, but I want my peace of mind. I must tell you I have been longing for the return of my peace of mind.

SISTER ALOYSIUS: You may not have it. It is not your place to be complacent. That's for the children. That's what we give them.

SISTER JAMES: I think I'm starting to understand you a little. But it's so unsettling to look at things and people with suspicion. It feels as if I'm less close to God.

SISTER ALOYSIUS: When you take a step to address wrongdoing, you are taking a step away from God but in His service. Dealing with such matters is hard and thankless work.

SISTER JAMES: I've become more reserved in class. I feel separated from the children.

SISTER ALOYSIUS: That's as it should be.

SISTER JAMES: But I feel. Wrong. And about this other matter, I don't have any evidence. I'm not at all certain that anything's happened.

SISTER ALOYSIUS: We can't wait for that.

SISTER JAMES: But what if it's nothing?

SISTER ALOYSIUS: Then it's nothing. I wouldn't mind being wrong. But I doubt I am.

SISTER JAMES: Then what's to be done?

SISTER ALOYSIUS: I don't know.

SISTER JAMES: You'll know what to do.

SISTER ALOYSIUS: I don't know what to do. There are parameters that protect him and hinder me.

SISTER JAMES: But he can't be safe if it's established. I doubt he could recover from the shame.

SISTER ALOYSIUS: What have you seen?

SISTER JAMES: I don't know.

SISTER ALOYSIUS: What have you seen?

SISTER JAMES: He took Donald to the rectory.

SISTER ALOYSIUS: What for?

SISTER JAMES: A talk.

SISTER ALOYSIUS: Alone?

SISTER JAMES: Yes.

SISTER ALOYSIUS: When?

SISTER JAMES: A week ago.

SISTER ALOYSIUS: Why didn't you tell me?

SISTER JAMES: I didn't think there was anything wrong with it. It never came into my mind that he . . . that there could be anything wrong.

SISTER ALOYSIUS: Of all the children. Donald Muller. I suppose it makes sense.

SISTER JAMES: How does it make sense?

SISTER ALOYSIUS: He's isolated. The little sheep lagging behind is the one the wolf goes for.

SISTER JAMES: I don't know that anything's wrong!

SISTER ALOYSIUS: Our first Negro student. I thought there'd be fighting, a parent or two to deal with . . . I should've foreseen this possibility.

SISTER JAMES: How could you imagine it?

SISTER ALOYSIUS: It is my job to outshine the fox in cleverness! That's my job!

SISTER JAMES: But maybe it's nothing!

SISTER ALOYSIUS: Then why do you look like you've seen the Devil?

SISTER JAMES: It's just the way the boy acted when he came back to class.

SISTER ALOYSIUS: He said something?

SISTER JAMES: No. It was his expression. He looked frightened and . . . he put his head on the desk in the most peculiar way. (*Struggles.*) And one other thing. I think there was alcohol on his breath. There was alcohol on his breath. (**SISTER ALOYSIUS** *looks toward the rectory.*)

SISTER ALOYSIUS: Eight years ago at St. Boniface we had a priest who had to be stopped. But I had Monsignor Scully then . . . who I could rely on. Here, there's no man I can go to, and men run everything. We are going to have to stop him ourselves.

SISTER JAMES: Can't you just . . . report your suspicions?

SISTER ALOYSIUS: To Monsignor Benedict? The man's guileless! He would just ask Father Flynn!

SISTER JAMES: Well, would that be such a bad idea?

SISTER ALOYSIUS: And he would believe whatever Father Flynn told him. He would think the matter settled.

SISTER JAMES: But maybe that is all that needs to be done. If it's true. If I had done something awful, and I was confronted with it, I'd be so repentant.

SISTER ALOYSIUS: Sister James, my dear, you must try to imagine a very different kind of person than yourself. A man who has done this has already denied a great deal. If I tell the monsignor and he is satisfied with Father Flynn's rebuttal, the matter is suppressed.

SISTER JAMES: Well then tell the bishop.

SISTER ALOYSIUS: The hierarchy of the Church does not permit my going to the bishop. No. Once I tell the Monsignor, it's out of my hands. I'm helpless. I'm going to have to come up with a pretext, get Father Flynn into my office. Try to force it. You'll have to be there.

SISTER JAMES: Me? No! Why? Oh no, Sister! I couldn't!

SISTER ALOYSIUS: I can't be closeted alone with a priest. Another Sister must be in attendance and it has to be you. The circle of confidence mustn't be made any wider. Think of the boy if this gets out.

SISTER JAMES: I can't do it!

SISTER ALOYSIUS: Why not? You're squeamish?

SISTER JAMES: I'm not equipped! It's . . . I would be embarrassed. I couldn't possibly be present if the topic were spoken of!

SISTER ALOYSIUS: Please, Sister, do not indulge yourself in witless adolescent scruples. I assure you I would prefer a more seasoned confederate. But you are the one who came to me.

SISTER JAMES: You told me to!

SISTER ALOYSIUS: Would you rather leave the boy to be exploited? And don't think this will be the only story. If you close your eyes, you will be a party to all that comes after.

SISTER JAMES: You're supposed to tell the monsignor!

SISTER ALOYSIUS: That you saw a look in a boy's eye? That *perhaps* you smelled something on his breath? Monsignor Benedict thinks the sun rises and sets on Father Flynn. You'd be branded a hysteric and transferred.

SISTER JAMES: We can ask him.

SISTER ALOYSIUS: Who?

SISTER JAMES: The boy. Donald Muller.

SISTER ALOYSIUS: He'll deny it.

SISTER JAMES: Why?

SISTER ALOYSIUS: Shame.

SISTER JAMES: You can't know that.

SISTER ALOYSIUS: And if he does point the finger, how do you think that will be received in this community? A black child. (*No answer.*) I am going to think this through. Then I'm going to invite Father Flynn to my office on an unrelated matter. You will be there.

Sister James: But what good can I do?

Sister Aloysius: Aside from the unacceptability of a priest and nun being alone, I need a witness.

Sister James: To what?

Sister Aloysius: He may tell the truth and lie afterwards. (**Sister James** *looks toward the rectory*.)

Sister James: The boys are coming out of the rectory. They look happy enough.

Sister Aloysius: They look smug. Like they have a secret.

Sister James: There he is.

Sister Aloysius: If I could, Sister James, I would certainly choose to live in innocence. But innocence can only be wisdom in a world without evil. Situations arise and we are confronted with wrongdoing and we need to act.

Sister James: I have to take the boys up to class.

Sister Aloysius: Go on, then. Take them. I will be talking to you.

FAT CHICKS

BY GUSTAVO OTT

MARTINA *used to work in* ANGELA'*s advertising agency but resigned when* SHE *learned of* ANGELA'*s criminal behavior with* HER *clients. This is the first time that* ANGELA *has spoken with* MARTINA *since* SHE *left the firm, and* SHE'*s astounded to learn that* MARTINA *has since "found religion." To* ANGELA, *however, the only things that still count for anything are sex and power. As the scene reaches its powerful climax at the end, the values of both characters are thrown into stark relief. The scene begins with* ANGELA *speaking directly to the audience, as* SHE *does throughout the play.*

ANGELA: (*To the audience.*) They say that the people who come face to face with death and escape are able to make their dreams come true. Maybe they find a meaning in life that the rest of us will only see when it's too late. Martina recovered from her suicide attempt. And a week later, I asked her to meet me at the bowling alley. To offer her a deal. To offer her a dignified retreat. At that time, and even now that it's all over with, I could never have imagined what that damned . . . roly-poly was capable of. (*To* MARTINA.) I asked you to meet me in a public place so you wouldn't be scared. Although this bowling alley is enough to give anyone the creeps. (*Sound of pins.*) What you did . . . the pills . . . it got to me. . . . (*Pins.*) Did you know that I dreamt about you that same night?

MARTINA: Guilty conscience.

ANGELA: Right, my conscience. I want to offer you a deal. (**MARTINA** *picks a ball and plays.*) I rescue your company. We clean it up. And we go back to the old system: you work on your own, but inside the agency. With me.

MARTINA: And what do I have to do?

ANGELA: (**SHE** *plays.*) Forget everything.

MARTINA: Just like that?

ANGELA: Of course.

MARTINA: What about Valerie?

ANGELA: She's expendable.

MARTINA: You'd fire her?

ANGELA: She's not important.

MARTINA: She won a Clio.

ANGELA: They win an award and then disappear—it's nothing new. Not everyone gets over success. Besides, everyone knows that you were the one who deserved the award, the idea was yours, ever since the toad everything's been yours. I promise the next award is yours. The next Clio goes to you. Your turn.

MARTINA: You know who I dreamt about that night?

ANGELA: What?

MARTINA: Guess who I dreamt about that night when I was dying.

ANGELA: I don't see what that has to do with. . . .

MARTINA: I dreamt about God. (**MARTINA** *bowls. Sounds of pins falling.*)

ANGELA: God?

MARTINA: It was God. And he told me: The good man disappears. Martina, all men deceive and manipulate. There's no sincerity anymore. In whom shall I place my trust?

ANGELA: What for?

MARTINA: And He said: Before you do anything, before you think about the consequences, before you think about what you want to get in this life, you must promise that you will do only what is good. The right thing.

ANGELA: The right thing for the company . . . right?

MARTINA: The right thing. What is good.

ANGELA: Turn me in? You know you can't. . . .

MARTINA: I'm not talking about that.

ANGELA: Then what are you talking about?

MARTINA: I'm going to do what's right, what should be done, what God wants me to do.

ANGELA: What, are you going to become a nun or something? What?

MARTINA: In my dream, God. . . .

ANGELA: Dream, what? What are you trying to tell me? Stop talking in parables. As far as I know God isn't interested in my company and all its little details and particulars. Or is he? Is he going to go into advertising now? Besides, how do you know it was him?

MARTINA: Angela. . . .

ANGELA: You talked to him, personally, he told you all this in words or symbols. . . .

MARTINA: When you. . . .

ANGELA: What? What? What the fuck are you trying to tell me?

MARTINA: The right thing.

ANGELA: Martina, look at me carefully. What the fuck do I care about the right thing?

MARTINA: The right thing is the closest thing to heaven. Angela . . . the right thing is more important than the recognition or the prestige or any accomplishment. God told me that and more.

ANGELA: What was it? The Sunday sermon?

MARTINA: He told me about eternity.

ANGELA: No kidding!

MARTINA: Eternity, he said, is what should be. Good.

ANGELA: And he told you what you're going to do?

MARTINA: Yes.

ANGELA: And that is . . . ?

MARTINA: To seek him.

ANGELA: Who, a cop?

MARTINA: Jesus.

ANGELA: God and all that?

MARTINA: Ahah.

ANGELA: What a bunch of crap! Are you fucking with me or what?

MARTINA: He will bring me salvation.

ANGELA: Right, but the money. Did God tell you where you're going to get the money to save your ass, to post your bail, pay the lawyers? It's all going to cost you.

MARTINA: Someday we'll all have to pay.

ANGELA: Sure, but it's a lot easier to pay when you got money in the bank, sweetheart. OK. I get it. You're going to implicate me. OK. OK. OK. (*Pause.*) You go to court, fine, in advertising, you're dead. Got it?

MARTINA: My character means more to me than my profession.

ANGELA: Right, but no one talks about you because you have character. Oh sure, you may feel good about yourself now thinking you've got a direct line to St. Peter, but forget it, when you're in jail, when you're out on the street, a fat chick on the street, a horrifying dinosaur with thyroid problems, like you looking for work and the doors just keep slamming in your face, then you'll know what character is.

MARTINA: Character means doing what's right.

ANGELA: No one wants to hear about the people who did the right thing and failed. Forget it. In this world there are five billion nobodies with principles, but if they vanish from the face of the earth, who cares? Sweetheart, it's just that evil gets more attention than good. It's a mental thing. Good things just aren't interesting, the only good things that are worthwhile are sex and power. And you know why? Because when they're good they're very good but when they're bad they're better.

MARTINA: I'd rather fail and be at peace and proud of myself.

ANGELA: I'll see you teaching classes in a university, good God, what humiliation, an advertising exec teaching classes and earning as little as any professor. That's sickening. It makes my skin crawl.

MARTINA: Someday you'll find out that power and money aren't everything and it may just so happen that you have them, but they'll never bring you happiness.

ANGELA: As far as your XXX-rated dream about God goes, just let me say this, life isn't like the movies, sugar. And God bless you . . . you bitch.

MARTINA: If you see Valerie tell her I forgive her.

ANGELA: (*Explodes.*) *WHAT A WUSS!! WHAT A WIMP YOU TURNED INTO!!!* "I forgive her." Who the hell do you think you are, fatso, the mother of God? So don't come spouting that litany for prisoners and suicides to me. Good-bye and go lose yourself in paradise if that'll make you happy. I don't want to see you ever again. (**ANGELA** *turns to leave. Suddenly* **SHE** *stops.*) Actually, some of the things you said. . . .

MARTINA: They touched you?

ANGELA: No, but I bet you could make a good commercial out of that garbage. I'm going to get some use out of your words, especially that bit about God and character, eternity, and all that crap. It will work like a charm in a commercial for the new Ford trucks. (*Exits. Pause.* **MARTINA** *continues looking at the audience.*)

MARTINA: It's a good idea. But it'll work better with Japanese trucks. Don't you think?

IN THE NEXT ROOM OR THE VIBRATOR PLAY
BY SARAH RUHL

The setting is late nineteenth-century America. MRS. GIVINGS, *a well-off doctor's wife, has hired an African-American woman,* ELIZABETH, *as a wet nurse for her infant.* ELIZABETH'*s child, Henry, recently died from cholera, and* SHE *still has plenty of milk, so* SHE *has agreed to nurse the Givings child. But recently, one of* MRS. GIVINGS'*s guests, a young artist who created a painting of Elizabeth nursing the baby, made a pass at his model—who was greatly shocked because* SHE'*s a married woman. In the following scene,* ELIZABETH *has come to give notice, but as the situation develops,* SHE *fails to suppress* HER *bitterness any longer and finally vents* HER *true feelings about relying on God.*

MRS. GIVINGS: Elizabeth. I did not expect you. What is it?

ELIZABETH: Mrs. Givings, I came to tell you that today was my last day working for you. My husband doesn't like me gone so much. He wants me home with my own children.

MRS. GIVINGS: But you can't leave us, Elizabeth! What on earth will we do without you?

ELIZABETH: She is almost ready to have cow's milk. Or a little bit of rice porridge.

MRS. GIVINGS: I suppose. I was not thinking only of the food. (ELIZABETH *nods slowly*.) But why today? I don't understand.

ELIZABETH: Mr. Irving insisted on walking me home. He was not—inappropriate—but he kept hold of my arm. He paid me a large sum of money—for the sitting. And he walked me up to my front door.

MRS. GIVINGS: Oh, dear.

ELIZABETH: My husband was home. My husband saw him. And me. And the painting.

MRS. GIVINGS: Oh! Was your husband very angry? About the painting?

ELIZABETH: The painting? No. He cried when he saw the painting. It's your hands, he said. Mr. Irving must be a good painter, it's hard to paint hands. But he doesn't want me working here, not anymore.

MRS. GIVINGS: Of course. Yes—I understand.

ELIZABETH: No—you don't. (*A pause*.) I'll just say good-bye to Lotty. I have grown fond of her.

MRS. GIVINGS: Yes. Well. She is in the nursery. She is fat and happy, all thanks to you. Elizabeth—how old was your Henry Douglas when he died?

ELIZABETH: Twelve weeks.

MRS. GIVINGS: What did he die of?

ELIZABETH: Cholera.

MRS. GIVINGS: I am sorry.

ELIZABETH: Thank you.

Mrs. Givings: I think I should die of sorrow, in your place.

Elizabeth: Die of sorrow? A mother of two cannot die of sorrow.

Mrs. Givings: But how do you go on, after?

Elizabeth: My mother told me to pray each day since I was a little girl, to pray that you borrow everything, everyone you love, from God. That way your heart doesn't break when you have to give your son, or your mother, or your husband, back to God. I prayed Jesus, let me be humble. I borrowed my child, I borrowed my husband, I borrowed my own life from you, God. But he felt like mine not like God's, he felt like mine, more mine than anything. God must have this huge horrible cabinet—all the babies who get returned—and all those babies inside, they're all crying even with God Himself to rock them to sleep, still they want their mothers. So when I started to feel something for this baby, for your baby, I thought no, take her back, God. When I first met her all I could think was: she is alive and Henry is not. I had all this milk—I wished it would dry up. Just get through the year, I thought. Your milk will dry up and you will forget. The more healthy your baby got, the more dead my baby became. I thought of her like a tic. I thought—fill her up and then pop! You will see the blood of my Henry underneath. But she seemed so grateful for the milk. Sometimes I hated her for it. But she would look at me, she would give me this look—I do not know what to call it if it is not called love. I hope every day you keep her—you keep her close to you—and you remember the blood that her milk was made from. The blood of my son, my Henry. Good-bye, Mrs. Givings.

Mrs. Givings: Good-bye, Elizabeth.

THROWN BY ANGELS
BY GWENDOLYN SCHWINKE

BABY *has run away from* HER *father's house and has been missing for two nights. For the past seven years,* BABY'S *father has kept* BABY *and* HER *sister,* SISSY, *locked in the basement, telling* THEM *the world was destroyed by fire, reading the Bible to* THEM, *and committing incest with both. This amusing scene is filled with discoveries as* BABY *excitedly reports to* SISSY *what* SHE *has found outside* THEIR *basement, and struggles to persuade* SISSY *to run away with* HER. SISSY *resists* HER *arguments, struggling to maintain* HER *naïve faith in* THEIR *father—until the very end of the scene, when the prospect of boys and burgers wins* HER *over. On one level, the situation appears very humorous, but on a much deeper level, it will lead* THEM *to confront the nightmare of* THEIR *relationship with* THEIR *father, cause* THEM *to lose* THEIR *religious faith, and thrust* THEM *into a long and painful search for* THEIR *own identities.*

BABY: It's out there.

SISSY: Baby, you're back, thank God. We thought you were dead.

BABY: Did you hear me? It's out there.

SISSY: Daddy just left. He went out to look for you.

BABY: I know, I saw him go. I was hiding in the bushes.

SISSY: He's gonna be really mad about that.

BABY: I don't care, I don't care about him. Stop talking about him. Listen to me: it is out there.

SISSY: What? What is out there?

BABY: The world! The whole world is out there.

SISSY: Well of course it's out there. The world has been burnt, the world has been scorched, but it's still out there. It's not like the fire ate away the whole planet and we're sitting on some little chunk of rock hurtling through space.

BABY: No, I mean it's out there just like it was. Trees, grass, birds. . . .

SISSY: Well, Baby, things grow back. Remember Noah? The great flood? God's green earth will be renewed. That's the whole point—

BABY: There's people.

SISSY: There are not.

BABY: Are too.

SISSY: You're telling me you saw people?

BABY: I did.

SISSY: Maybe they were angels. Or devils. Daddy told us long ago, that after the fire angels and devils shall roam the earth. It's a dangerous time. That was the very reason, in case you forgot, that we were not supposed to leave the basement. You just saw some devils. You're lucky they didn't eat you up.

BABY: They gave me something.

SISSY: They did not. . . . What?

BABY: A cheeseburger.

Sissy: You are making that up!

Baby: And I ate it.

Sissy: You ate it? You ate food given you by devils? You're gonna turn to stone or burst into flames or something.

Baby: They weren't devils, they were just regular people. They were nice to me.

Sissy: Baby, what are you thinking with? The devil is always nice. That's the way he operates.

Baby: Sissy, two nights ago when I ran off, I was so scared. You know I haven't been out of this basement since we came here seven years ago. But I couldn't help myself. That night I looked over at him and I could not stand it, I could not stand to be next to him, I could not stand to be in this house any more. The window was open there in his room. Just the screen was on it, and outside, I could see outside. Upstairs there he has windows and some wind was coming in and I could see some trees. He went to sleep, and I just looked out that window, and smelled, and listened. Something was out there. So I stood up on the bed and I took a couple of big bounces, and I jumped right at that screen. It crashed away, and I was out! I was on the ground, and I just ran as fast as I could into the woods.

Sissy: I heard that, I was awake down here and I heard the noise. Did he come after you? He did, didn't he?

Baby: He did, but out there the trees are thick, and I'm littler than him. I'm faster, he couldn't catch me and I just kept running. He kept screaming that I wouldn't make it, that the world was ended and I wouldn't last, but this thought happened to me, Sissy, this thought—

SISSY: What?

BABY: This thought just popped into my head like something you'd see in those little bubbles in the funny papers. Remember that? Remember the funny papers? Where people talk in bubbles? I don't know why I remembered the bubbles, but I did, and this is the thing that was in my bubble: Fuck You! And then I said it out loud. And I realized that it was a prayer. It's not a prayer you kneel for—it's a prayer you pray when you're running. So for hours and hours I ran, and I prayed: Fuck You.

SISSY: Baby, that'll send you straight to hell.

BABY: Yeah, maybe, but listen to what happened. After a long while I got too tired to run, and I got really too tired to even be scared. I just went to sleep there on the ground, in the dark. And when I woke up it was light—the sun was coming up, and it was so beautiful. The sky was all purply-blue and it was turning white over where the sun was . . . and I started looking around me and seeing all this stuff. And that's when I realized: the world is still out there! Trees and grass and wind and birds—

SISSY: Things grow back. . . .

BABY: These were big trees, I'm telling you, really old, big trees. Older than seven years.

SISSY: It could have been a trick, a miracle. . . .

BABY: They were just regular old trees. I got up and I started walking to the sun. I walked all day, until I got under where the sun was in the sky, and I passed it up and kept walking. About the time it got dark, I started to hear noises. Frogs. . . .

SISSY: Oh, no. . . .

Baby: No, it was good, and then a whippoorwill! Remember whippoorwills? I heard one, and then I heard this soft rushing, like the wind, but different. So I followed the sound, and then I saw a light, in the distance. It was orange, and kind of glowing, and I went towards it.

Sissy: Baby, I know you're a genius and everything, but sometimes you act like you don't have a brain in your head—

Baby: And when I got closer, there was less trees and the noise was really loud, like a roaring—

Sissy: Oh, Baby, how could you do something as—

Baby: And it was a highway. With cars. And lights. And right there by the highway, was my big orange glow. It was a sign.

Sissy: A sign of the devil.

Baby: No. Burger King. (*Holds out a paper bag.*) I brought one for you. I ate one, nothing happened to me. This one's yours, a big, fat, flame-broiled Whopper. It took me a day to remember my way back, so it's cold now, but you can still smell it. I started out with some fries, too, but I couldn't help myself.

Sissy: (*Unable to resist the temptation,* **She** *rips into the burger and speaks with* **Her** *mouth full.*) It's real! This is the real thing!

Baby: The world isn't over. It's all out there. Hamburgers, cars, people, television, music, computers. They still have it. It's just like it was before. He lied to us.

Sissy: He would never lie to us. Why would he lie? What earthly reason would he have for lying to us about the end of the world?

Baby: Sissy. (*Pause.*) There's boys.

Sissy: Boys?

Baby: Boys. (*Short pause while* **Sissy** *considers this.*)

Sissy: All right. Let's go!

CELL CYCLE
BY CRISTINA PIPPA

This scene deftly tracks a growing sense of bonding between two sisters following the death of THEIR parents. (The next scene from the same play revisits the two women later in time.) ALICIA, the older, is a research scientist, and has been caring for THEIR father, who is dying from a terminal disease. SHE really does care for CAITLYN, despite the latter's failure as a caregiver and HER obsession with Christianity. The scene becomes very emotional as it develops, particularly toward the end, as ALICIA begins to understand what drove HER sister to the comfort of traditional religious faith.

CAITLYN: Have I been mean lately? I feel like I've been mean lately.

ALICIA: I don't know.

CAITLYN: 'Cause we're all sinners, and I know I'm never going to be perfect.

ALICIA: I didn't say you did anything.

CAITLYN: I just—can you give me grace?

ALICIA: I never say grace.

CAITLYN: I mean I want to ask for your forgiveness.

ALICIA: Sure. You've got it.

Caitlyn: Are you okay?

Alicia: I guess I'm a little down. Like I just watched *Mystic Pizza* or something.

Caitlyn: It was on TV?

Alicia: No. I didn't watch it. I just feel like I did.

Caitlyn: *Mystic Pizza*'s not depressing. You're thinking of *St. Elmo's Fire*.

Alicia: Have you seen *Mystic Pizza*? They're totally different.

Caitlyn: We should watch *Troop Beverly Hills*. That'll cheer you up! Remember when we used to watch it all the time? Now we're leaving such busy lives. We hardly get to see each other.

Alicia: Leading. I think the expression is "leading busy lives."

Caitlyn: Leaving, too. We're leaving sooner than we think. But it's okay. Some people really worry about death. But we're not so much dying as leaving. Leaving this strange place where people fight and sin—to go home.

Alicia: Why are you telling me this?

Caitlyn: I know you're really worried about Dad.

Alicia: You're not?

Caitlyn: Of course. But also not.

Alicia: It must be nice to have so little weighing you down.

Caitlyn: 'Cause God wants us to give all our cares to Him, to let Him carry our burdens. Dad should do that. And you should, too, Alicia. (**She** *waits for a response.*) I could help you.

ALICIA: I'm almost finished.

CAITLYN: I mean help you find God.

ALICIA: Yeah, you're so helpful. Why didn't you take Dad to the doctor so he wouldn't have to go by himself?

CAITLYN: He always goes by himself.

ALICIA: This was a bigger deal.

CAITLYN: I had Bible study with my friends. He said it was fine. And you weren't there.

ALICIA: I'm working!

CAITLYN: It's no wonder you're depressed. You don't have God and you're working in a morgue.

ALICIA: Next to a morgue. I'm working in a lab.

CAITLYN: Whatever.

ALICIA: And since you're not working, you should take care of Dad. Spend time with him. Get him to go out to lunch.

CAITLYN: You're right. I haven't done as much as I should. (*Pause, while* SHE *thinks.*) You know, there was a guy who made it his goal to think about God as much as possible. It's really hard. Even when I jog, I end up thinking about what I'm going to wear when I go out.

ALICIA: But you do think of God all the time.

CAITLYN: I try.

ALICIA: To the point where you might be missing things because He's—

CAITLYN: Missing what?

ALICIA: Anything. God's all you think about and whenever you're not thinking of Him, you're thinking about not thinking of Him, which means you're still thinking of Him.

CAITLYN: Don't you think about science all the time?

ALICIA: Uhmm. Well, I do a lot, but I'm not sure as intensely. Maybe.

CAITLYN: God and church and Younglife—they're just as important to me. I know they're not to you.

ALICIA: Yeah, and they never were. That's what I wonder about. Is it true there's a God-gene?

CAITLYN: What's that?

ALICIA: A gene that makes you more likely to be religious? Some geneticists say they've found it.

CAITLYN: I don't think so.

ALICIA: Then why do you think we have such . . . different beliefs? We had the same parents.

CAITLYN: I know why I need God. Sometimes I wish you did, too, but I know that everyone has their moment.

ALICIA: You remember a moment? (CAITLYN *nods*.) When was it?

CAITLYN: When I found out Mom was sick and was probably going to die. I was little, but I still remember. I lay down on that fuzzy rug in my room and I just cried and cried and cried. You couldn't stop me.

ALICIA: I remember that.

CAITLYN: And it was Sunday, so Mom took me to the Youth Group that night. I'd been there before, but I never. . . . I just remember all these kids being so happy to see me. And one of them had just lost her dad. You know Sarah Brendan? Her dad had a heart attack at work and her Mom was the Youth Minister and was so nice to me. She was like Super Mom, you know. I even thought maybe she'd marry Dad some day.

ALICIA: Eewww.

CAITLYN: Yeah, that was dumb. She was kind of old. But I just felt like everything was okay that night. That if God needed Mom like He needed Sarah's dad, that would be okay with me. Suddenly the world made sense.

ALICIA: I can see that.

CELL CYCLE
BY CRISTINA PIPPA

This scene occurs later in the same play, but here it is ALICIA *who is wrestling with* HER *loss and* CAITLYN *who emerges the stronger of the two.* CAITLYN *has since lost* HER *preachy religiosity, and* THEIR *father has just passed away;* THEY *are now parentless, and the reality of that situation is hitting them. While reflecting traditional views of death and heaven, the scene actually focuses on more important questions that always lie beyond the skills of the "Pastor Owens" in our lives: Where do we go from here? What is our new identity without any parents? What is our new relationship as "siblings alone"?*

CAITLYN: He died, Alicia. After surgery, Dad . . . passed on. (*Pause.*) Do you want a hug or . . . something? I wanted one. When it happened there were all these people from Dad's work and Pastor Owen wasn't there yet. I mean, when he got there I felt so much better. But before I was looking around and I was like . . . wow . . . we have no family. There's no one here. And I know Dad told you to go and you wanted to work, but I was kind of mad to be there by myself. I was like . . . why can't she do whatever she's doing later? Why am I here by myself? I'm too young to watch my Dad die by myself. So I'm sorry. I shouldn't have thought that stuff. (*Pause.*) Uhmmm . . . you're still not saying anything.

ALICIA: I still can't believe he's dead. It's totally . . . out of the realm of possibility . . . to me. Even though—

CAITLYN: I know.

ALICIA: I know it happened. I know you're standing there telling me this, but you don't even look that sad. (**SHE** *begins to cry.*)

CAITLYN: I am, really.

ALICIA: It's okay. You know what? I'm not that sad. About Dad, I mean. I'm crying but it's because I miss Mom. She was everything. And now, I don't know.

CAITLYN: You can miss Mom, too.

ALICIA: I know I can. I do. I really . . . hurt. But I can't miss him because I don't feel like he's gone. I feel like he can't be 'cause he was always there. I can still see him . . . and I can't really see her. She's just more gone now.

CAITLYN: I hate to tell you this, Alicia, but he is gone. I was there so I can tell you it.

ALICIA: I know.

CAITLYN: And you weren't there. And it wasn't beautiful at all. His lips were cracked and his breath was making me feel sick. His last breath. It was really loud and smelled strange and I felt like I should kiss his cheek but I couldn't 'cause I was too creeped-out by my own dad. So no one kissed his cheek. You would have. I know that. You wouldn't have been scared.

ALICIA: I would. I'm scared now. I should be trying to make you feel better but I have nothing.

CAITLYN: Pastor Owen did. Really. I'm okay. What he said helped so much. And I don't know if you would like it, or whatever.

ALICIA: You can tell me.

CAITLYN: He said Dad's body is just a . . . I don't know . . . a shell. And his soul went to heaven, but little . . . uhmmm . . . I guess bits of it are still here, like attached to my soul and attached to your soul. Mom's too.

ALICIA: How do we know he went to heaven? If it's really his fault that people died, that he didn't pay enough attention, or respond—

CAITLYN: I don't believe it was his fault. I know he was human but I guess it's like another sort of faith for me that he was good. Maybe it's naive.

ALICIA: It's not. Maybe I made Mom out to be too good. It just means we loved them. And I don't know that anything was his fault. I hope it wasn't.

CAITLYN: It was really hard for me to come here. I didn't know where the room was. I had to ask, like seven people. And I saw that morgue you were talking about. It's really creepy. Just to know it's there.

ALICIA: Thank you. For coming to tell me in person.

CAITLYN: I wish everything was the same as it used to be.

ALICIA: Like when?

CAITLYN: Like when we were kids. I miss being the four of us in that house. How did you get over Mom dying?

ALICIA: How did you?

CAITLYN: I was young. I guess I am still.

ALICIA: I don't know that I ever did get over it. If I did, maybe because we had Dad. And he had us. Remember how we slept in their bed that night? You on one side of Dad and me on the other? I was the only one who cried.

CAITLYN: That night.

ALICIA: I really believed in God then. I pictured Mom up in heaven. Eating pizza, I think. Dad said to look up at the stars and see her.

CAITLYN: To me, too. Yeah. This is much harder than I imagined.

ALICIA: Yeah.

CAITLYN: You know, in half a second, there were all these people from Dad's work, people I never met. I was like . . . supposed to put myself together.

ALICIA: I doubt anyone expected that.

CAITLYN: They kept asking what the arrangements were going to be.

ALICIA: Arrangements.

CAITLYN: What?

ALICIA: You said—

CAITLYN: I don't want to look at coffins.

ALICIA: I don't either.

CAITLYN: Pastor Owen's going to help.

ALICIA: I guess we should go.

CAITLYN: This place is so real-looking. I mean . . . you know what I mean? Like a mad scientist's laboratory in the movies, except it's real.

ALICIA: I was so excited about working here. About finding something. I don't even know what I was looking for. Or why I thought I would find it.

CAITLYN: You have to come back here, okay?

ALICIA: Why?

CAITLYN: Dad was bragging to one of his war buddies when you went to get dinner last night—about how you were going to find the cure for cancer. So other people wouldn't have to go through it. (ALICIA *gives* CAITLYN *a long hug.*) He seems nice, Alicia.

ALICIA: Who?

CAITLYN: Your boyfriend.

ALICIA: Oh. Thanks.

GIDION'S KNOT
BY JOHNNA ADAMS

HEATHER *is the teacher of a student who committed suicide just four days ago after an incident at the school;* CORRYN *is the boy's mother. The scene takes place in* HEATHER'*s classroom after school. When a character's name is followed by an ellipsis (e.g.,* "HEATHER: . . . ."), *this indicates a nonverbal response to the previous line. The ellipsis line may be played in many ways: as a pause, a beat, a look, a movement, a silence, a smile, or a sudden thought—or it can just be used to give the scene some air, some room, some tension, and the like. A slash (/) in the middle of a character's line indicates an interruption. The next speaking character should begin her line where the slash appears. Beyond this challenge of the text transcription, the scene's structure is also challenging because there is no central climax. The action unfolds through a series of minor conflicts as each character grapples with the death of a child. The essay to which the teacher refers can be found in the* Monologues for Women *section of this anthology.*

HEATHER: Yes? (*Another knock. The knocker can't hear* HER *through the door.* SHE *goes to the door and looks out through a small window.* SHE *opens the door.*) Yes? (CORRYN FELL *enters hesitantly.*) Are you looking / for . . . ?

CORRYN: I have a parent-teacher conference. Is / this— . . . ?

HEATHER: Do you know the room?

CORRYN: I thought . . .—

HEATHER: If you go to the office and speak to the office manager she can tell you which room you're looking for. Just give her the teacher's name.

CORRYN: The office manager?

HEATHER: Carole. She's at the desk.

CORRYN: Thank you.

HEATHER: All right. (CORRYN *goes out.* HEATHER *returns to* HER *desk.* SHE *stares at* HER *phone. Another knock, then* CORRYN *pokes* HER *head back in cautiously.*)

CORRYN: I'm sorry. The office?

HEATHER: It's down the hall and to your left—at the end of the hall there.

CORRYN: Oh. Okay. Thank you. (CORRYN *leaves.* HEATHER *stands for a long moment in the middle of the room.* SHE *goes back to grading papers. Something breaks inside* HER. SHE *stops and puts* HER *head in* HER *hands, taking deep breaths, almost hyperventilating, trying not to sob.* SHE *shakes* HER *head, and under* HER *breath.*)

HEATHER: God . . . oh God . . . God. . . (SHE *gets up and walks around the room.* SHE *picks up* HER *cell phone and puts it down.* SHE *almost has herself under control. A knock at the door.*) Oh God. (SHE *crosses to the door as* CORRYN *comes back in.*)

CORRYN: I'm / sorry—

HEATHER: Down the hall and to your left—

CORRYN: I found it. I found Carole.

HEATHER: You need directions to the room?

CORRYN: You're very helpful, aren't you? I mean you're irritated and not very good at hiding it but still . . .

HEATHER: . . . .

CORRYN: I'm sorry. That came out— . . .

HEATHER: Yes. It did.

CORRYN: . . . .

HEATHER: Do you need help finding the room?

CORRYN: No, I found the room.

HEATHER: No one was there? If you ask Carole—

CORRYN: This is the room.

HEATHER: No. No, I don't—

CORRYN: Four eighteen.

HEATHER: No, I don't have anything.

CORRYN: Two-thirty. I'm a little late.

HEATHER: I don't have anything scheduled.

CORRYN: Yes. I wrote it down. (**CORRYN** *pulls a rumpled piece of paper out of* **HER** *purse.*) Two-thirty. April fifth. Room four eighteen. Mrs. Clark.

HEATHER: . . . .

CORRYN: You're Mrs. Clark.

HEATHER: Yes.

CORRYN: I set it up. Here— (**CORRYN** *gives* **HEATHER** *the paper.*)

HEATHER: That's strange, I—I'm sorry.

CORRYN: That's all right. You forgot, I guess.

HEATHER: . . . .

CORRYN: I can come back. You're unprepared, I can see that.

HEATHER: No, it's fine. Come in.

CORRYN: Thank you very much. And thank you for making time.

HEATHER: I don't think you were at open house.

CORRYN: No.

HEATHER: . . . .

CORRYN: I set it up with Carole, I guess. I called her. Friday afternoon.

HEATHER: About?

CORRYN: About my son.

HEATHER: Who is your son?

CORRYN: Gidion.

HEATHER: . . . .

CORRYN: . . . .

HEATHER: . . . .

CORRYN: . . . .

HEATHER: . . . oh God . . .

CORRYN: We set up a parent-teacher conference. The principal was supposed to come, too.

HEATHER: . . . .

CORRYN: I guess she forgot.

HEATHER: No. Of course not. It's just— . . .

CORRYN: . . . .

HEATHER: . . . .

CORRYN: I missed open house. So we never got to meet.

HEATHER: You're Gidion's mother. Mrs. Gibson.

CORRYN: No. That was his father's name. Ms. Fell.

HEATHER: Mrs. Fell.

CORRYN: You can call me Corryn.

HEATHER: . . . .

CORRYN: You sent a note home with my son. Asking to meet with me.

HEATHER: Mrs. Fell.

CORRYN: Telling me he was suspended.

HEATHER: . . . .

CORRYN: There was a voice mail message, too . . . Saying to call.

HEATHER: . . . .

CORRYN: And I called and set something up. I guess with Carole maybe. Someone in the office. She didn't tell you?

HEATHER: No, she did.

CORRYN: You forgot.

HEATHER: . . . .

CORRYN: Well. We set this up.

HEATHER: Yes.

CORRYN: So here I am.

HEATHER: . . . .

CORRYN: . . . .

HEATHER: Mrs. Fell—

CORRYN: No, it's Ms.

HEATHER: Ms. Fell.

CORRYN: You can call me Corryn. If you'd like.

HEATHER: I'm so sorry. I'm so sorry. I'm so very, very sorry.

CORRYN: Thank you.

HEATHER: I didn't forget. I just . . . I didn't think you'd—

CORRYN: You sent a note home with my son. And left a message. Asking to meet with me. How could I not come?

HEATHER: . . . .

CORRYN: He's my son.

HEATHER: . . . .

CORRYN: You look pale. Have I given you a shock?

HEATHER: Oh God.

CORRYN: I didn't mean to.

HEATHER: . . . .

CORRYN: We did have an appointment.

HEATHER: . . . .

CORRYN: . . . .

HEATHER: . . . .

CORRYN: What did you want to talk about?

HEATHER: . . . .

CORRYN: About my son?

HEATHER: . . . .

CORRYN: Was it his grades?

HEATHER: . . . .

CORRYN: Attendance? Excessive tardiness? Running in the halls?

HEATHER: I don't . . .

CORRYN: I'd really like to know. I've been wondering. Your note was vague. The voice mail was cryptic. I've been up for about seventy-two hours. I can't sleep. I can't sleep because I've been playing this conversation out over and over again in my mind, wondering how it will go. You were more vocal in these little fantasies. You contributed. You explained . . . I don't know why you . . . did this to him. I don't know what happened.

HEATHER: . . . .

CORRYN: He looked devastated. When he handed me the note. He was shaking. He—

HEATHER: God! . . . oh God . . .

CORRYN: . . . .

HEATHER: . . . God . . .

CORRYN: I'm sorry.

HEATHER: I don't know / what—

CORRYN: I didn't mean—

HEATHER: God. / I just—

CORRYN: Would you like me to get you some water?

HEATHER: I didn't think— . . .

CORRYN: You look bloodless.

HEATHER: I didn't think you'd keep the appointment. It never occurred to me that you would keep the appointment.

CORRYN: He's my son.

HEATHER: I took it out of my calendar.

CORRYN: I see.

HEATHER: I didn't think you'd—

CORRYN: Well, I did.

HEATHER: I didn't think you'd still want to talk about—

CORRYN: About my son?

HEATHER: That it might be painful to . . .

CORRYN: Yes?

HEATHER: To talk about him so soon after his death.

CORRYN: . . . .

HEATHER: . . . .

CORRYN: . . . .

HEATHER: . . . .

CORRYN: Well.

HEATHER: . . . .

CORRYN: We had an appointment.

HEATHER: . . . .

CORRYN: . . . .

HEATHER: Yes, okay.

CORRYN: Good.

HEATHER: I'm really very sorry—

CORRYN: You've said so.

HEATHER: . . . .

CORRYN: Thank you . . . I'm sorry I missed open house. Gidion's father is dead. I'm a single mother. Getting a babysitter on a school night is like squeezing milk from stones. Do you have children?

HEATHER: No.

CORRYN: Oh . . . I never thought I would either. Pets?

HEATHER: What?

CORRYN: Do you have pets?

HEATHER: I'm not sure how I can help you, Ms. Fell.

CORRYN: Corryn, please. This doesn't have to be adversarial. Does it?

HEATHER: . . . .

CORRYN: How long have you been teaching?

HEATHER: Two years.

CORRYN: Really? You don't look young enough to be right out of school. You must have had a career before this, am I right?

HEATHER: Yes.

CORRYN: What was it?

HEATHER: I was in advertising.

CORRYN: And you got sick of making all that money and wanted to make a difference.

HEATHER: . . . .

CORRYN: Good for you.

HEATHER: Maybe we should reschedule. Find a time when the principal can join us.

CORRYN: Maybe she's just running late.

HEATHER: You should be with family now.

CORRYN: I'm exactly where I should be.

HEATHER: . . . .

CORRYN: . . . .

HEATHER: Okay.

CORRYN: You sent a note home with my son.

HEATHER: Yes.

CORRYN: You suspended him. Five days.

HEATHER: Yes.

CORRYN: He was fighting with another boy.

HEATHER: No.

CORRYN: He came home bruised. With dried blood on his mouth.

HEATHER: I don't know anything about that. That must have happened after he left school.

CORRYN: Was he beat up a lot? Picked on?

HEATHER: I never saw that happen.

CORRYN: But the day he was suspended he was beaten up. You didn't know?

HEATHER: I'm not surprised.

CORRYN: You're not?

HEATHER: . . . .

CORRYN: I was.

HEATHER: . . . .

CORRYN: . . . ?

HEATHER: He made some of the children angry.

CORRYN: And you. He made you angry.

HEATHER: Yes.

CORRYN: . . . .

HEATHER: . . . .

CORRYN: This isn't what I expected.

HEATHER: . . . .

CORRYN: That was very honest.

HEATHER: . . . .

CORRYN: He made you angry.

HEATHER: . . . .

CORRYN: Okay.

HEATHER: . . . .

CORRYN: This is nice. Your room. Colorful.

HEATHER: Thank you.

CORRYN: It's warm.

HEATHER: Thank you.

CORRYN: I envisioned a barren tomb. Painted prison green. Desks in depressing rows. Hard tile flooring that your heels made ominous clicking noises against as you paced up and down the rows, stroking the black thin hairs and warts covering your thick, bovine neck. A lovingly framed portrait of Stalin at the front of the room for the children to genuflect before as they file in.

HEATHER: I sent it out to be cleaned.

CORRYN: That's funny. You surprise me, too.

HEATHER: . . . .

CORRYN: What did you imagine I was like?

HEATHER: . . . .

CORRYN: You must have little mental images of all the parents. What they're like.

HEATHER: . . . .

CORRYN: Do I surprise you?

HEATHER: I knew you were a single mother.

CORRYN: How?

HEATHER: A writing project I gave. I asked them to describe their father.

CORRYN: He had nothing to write about.

HEATHER: He wrote about his grandfather instead.

CORRYN: He never met either grandfather. He made it up.

HEATHER: No. He wrote about what he imagined his grandfather's corpse was like. In the earth.

CORRYN: Well, that's original. I bet you never had a paper like it in all your two years of teaching.

HEATHER: No.

CORRYN: Is that when you began to hate him?

HEATHER: . . . .

CORRYN: Come on.

HEATHER: I didn't hate him.

CORRYN: Come on.

HEATHER: I didn't hate him.

CORRYN: Honestly?

HEATHER: I did not hate him.

CORRYN: Liar.

HEATHER: Ms. Fell. I think you should leave.

CORRYN: It's all right. I'm not angry about it. For Christ's sake. I don't like everyone I meet or everyone I know. I freely hate some of them. It isn't their fault. It just happens that way. I'm sure Gidion was the same. I'm sure you're the same.

HEATHER: I don't think this is accomplishing anything.

CORRYN: And in return, I don't expect everyone I meet to like me. I hated some of my teachers. My fifth grade teacher, in fact.

HEATHER: It's too soon for this.

CORRYN: I feel certain she hated me too.

HEATHER: Let's reschedule for a time when the principal and the school counselor can join us.

CORRYN: I don't expect you to like each and every one of your students, that would be inhuman.

HEATHER: I'll walk you to your car.

CORRYN: He hated you. It just happens sometimes.

HEATHER: . . . .

CORRYN: . . . .

HEATHER: You should take some time to grieve before . . . this. We should all take some time—

CORRYN: What did you mean when you said we should reschedule for a time when the principal can join us? Is the principal not able to join us?

HEATHER: I'm sure she thought that you wouldn't feel up to this discussion at this time.

CORRYN: Or that it no longer mattered.

HEATHER: That it might be in poor taste.

CORRYN: That this conversation no longer mattered.

HEATHER: That it wasn't the priority at the moment. Your grief is the priority.

CORRYN: We had an appointment.

HEATHER: . . . .

CORRYN: And no one cancelled it. You didn't cancel it.

HEATHER: . . . .

CORRYN: I would appreciate it if the principal would join us.

HEATHER: . . . .

CORRYN: Please. . . .

HEATHER: . . . .

CORRYN: Excuse me?

HEATHER: She's taking a personal day today.

CORRYN: That's what I thought you said.

HEATHER: She took the news about your son very hard.

CORRYN: . . . .

HEATHER: . . . .

CORRYN: Okay.

HEATHER: . . . .

CORRYN: Get her in here. Call her at home.

HEATHER: . . . .

CORRYN: . . . .

HEATHER: I'll talk to Carole. (**HEATHER** *goes out.* **CORRYN** *walks around the room.* **SHE** *reads some of the children's reports posted on the walls.* . . . **HEATHER** *re-enters.*) Carole spoke with her. She says she's on her way here.

CORRYN: Where does she live?

HEATHER: Not far. Fifteen minutes.

CORRYN: Good. I'll wait.

HEATHER: . . . .

CORRYN: . . . .

HEATHER: . . . .

CORRYN: Do you have that paper?

HEATHER: . . . ?

CORRYN: The one Gidion wrote about his grandfather? I saw some of them posted on the wall but not his.

HEATHER: I gave them back their papers. Except for the ones I posted.

CORRYN: Oh.

HEATHER: He didn't bring it home?

CORRYN: I don't know if he did.

HEATHER: You could check his book bag.

CORRYN: I'll do that.

HEATHER: Or his locker.

CORRYN: Where is it?

HEATHER: We'll call the facilities manager and he can take you to Gidion's locker and cut off the lock.

CORRYN: Thank you.

HEATHER: . . . .

CORRYN: . . . .

HEATHER: Or it might be here. In his desk. If he didn't take it home.

CORRYN: Which is his desk?

HEATHER: You're sitting in it.

CORRYN: Oh— . . . This? This is . . . ?

HEATHER: I assign them the seat they sit in on the first day of class. And you see it a lot during open house. The parents come in and choose the same seat.

CORRYN: Oh.

HEATHER: . . . .

CORRYN: How strange. (CORRYN *stands up and stares at the desk. When it is clear that* CORRYN *can't do it,* HEATHER *comes over and begins to take things out of the desk and lay them on the desktop. Corryn watches the items as they are revealed: two textbooks (math and social studies); a box of pencils and map pencils; a compass; a protractor; three folders with comic book superheroes on the cover; a spiral notebook; two stapled class assignments with "A+" written on them in red ink; and a folded note.* CORRYN *takes the note as* HEATHER *looks at the two writing assignments.* HEATHER *puts one of the papers in front of* CORRYN.)

HEATHER: It's this one. (**CORRYN** *opens and reads the note.*)

CORRYN: Who is Seneca?

HEATHER: She's a girl in my class. She sits behind Gidion.

CORRYN: She passes him notes.

HEATHER: Sometimes. She uses her phone and texts people the rest of the time.

CORRYN: Gidion doesn't have a phone, so I guess she had to do it old school. . . . Who names their daughter Seneca? That's as bad as Gidion. No wonder she liked him. She did like him?

HEATHER: Yes.

CORRYN: Did she have a crush on him?

HEATHER: I think she did.

CORRYN: A girl named Seneca sat behind Gidion and had a crush on him! She passed him notes because she couldn't text him! How wonderful. (*Reading from the note.*) This says, "Jake's a peehole. He's LYING like a peehole." Lying, all caps. "Don't get mad. That's what he wants. I believe you that he did it. I always believe YOU not that dicksnot." "You," all caps.

HEATHER: . . . .

CORRYN: She expresses herself well. Very clearly.

HEATHER: . . . .

CORRYN: I like her. She reminds me of me. They say boys always look for their mother in a mate. What does she look like?

HEATHER: She dyes her hair platinum blond and wears false eyelashes and a stuffed bra. She has a nose ring.

CORRYN: She's eleven?

HEATHER: Yes.

CORRYN: Wow . . . Wow.

HEATHER: . . . .

CORRYN: Did her parents have a parent-teacher conference with you at some point, too?

HEATHER: No.

CORRYN: Really?

HEATHER: . . . .

CORRYN: Okay. Lucky me then. Who's Jake?

HEATHER: He's a boy in the sixth grade.

CORRYN: Is he one of the children that Gidion made angry? On Friday? The day he died?

HEATHER: . . . .

CORRYN: There's a Jake on Facebook who made comments on Gidion's Facebook page over the weekend saying "You're a faggot" and "You're a lying faggot." After Gidion was dead, in fact, so— . . . untimely.

HEATHER: He couldn't have known Gidion was dead. The kids didn't know until this morning.

CORRYN: Oh, well, then.

HEATHER: It's not an excuse.

CORRYN: No, it's not.

HEATHER: . . . .

CORRYN: . . . .

HEATHER: Jake's been troubled lately. It's out of character if he did that.

CORRYN: You like Jake. He's the one that you like.

HEATHER: He's a good boy who has had a difficult year.

CORRYN: What did he think Gidion was lying about?

HEATHER: . . . .

CORRYN: . . . ?

HEATHER: We should wait for the principal.

CORRYN: . . . . All right.

HEATHER: . . . .

CORRYN: . . . .

SCENES FOR TWO MEN

GRACE

BY MICK GORDON
AND A. C. GRAYLING

A father-son talk over dinner about parenting, and the son's recent decision to join the priesthood, provides the occasion for TONY FRIEDMAN *to reveal some of* HIS *religious feelings to* HIS *Jewish son,* TOM. *This dinner table conversation offers a number of important discoveries for both characters during* THEIR *encounter; as a result, both characters emerge very different at the end of the scene than* THEY *were at the beginning.*

TOM: It's like saying, speaking English . . . we don't have to affirm our Englishness by denying French or Urdu. What do I want to deny other languages for? I want to see religions as languages for talking about the divine. And if you see them as languages, Christianity doesn't contradict Islam just as English doesn't contradict French.

TONY: But Christianity does contradict Islam, doesn't it? I mean Islam says Jesus was a minor prophet and Christianity says that he was the son of God. That sounds like a big difference to me.

TOM: I don't mean it like that. I'm not a literalist. I'm saying that the two religions are separate and equally valid approaches to dealing with the divine.

TONY: "The sigh of the oppressed creature, the heart of a heartless world, the soul of soulless conditions."

TOM: "The opium of the people."

TONY: Great man.

TOM: It's Mum's language I'm having trouble with.

TONY: Right.

TOM: It's why I'm always stuffed in conversations with her. Every point has a number. Everything must be clear. All problems answered by a league table. It's radical empiricism! I mean, do you really want to live in a world like that? I don't.

TONY: Oh dear . . .

TOM: Why do you love her so much?

TONY: Bloody good question.

TOM: I'm serious.

TONY: So am I.

TOM: Dad.

TONY: Fear.

TOM: Dad.

TONY: Really. A great aphrodisiac, fear.

TOM: Come on.

TONY: Admiration I think.

TOM: What?

Tony: Yeah. I've always admired your mother. It's true she has an unfortunate manner sometimes, but y'know, I've always thought she was right about stuff.

Tom: Really? Right?

Tony: Yeah. And her commitment. To what she believes, what she wants for the world. You know. Her hopes. You becoming a priest is genuinely very difficult for her.

Tom: I know. I've let her down.

Tony: No don't. Of course you haven't . . .

Tom: I couldn't stop myself.

Tony: Yeah. Well. It's important to you.

Tom: (*As a correction.*) Yes it is.

Tony: It'll be alright.

Tom: Will it?

Tony: We'll all go out for a curry. Take some ecstasy.

Tom: D'you remember that?

Tony: Every time I hear. You don't have any, do you?

Tom: What?

Tony: E.

Tom: No!

Tony: I'm only asking.

Tom: Dad! I'm going to be a priest!

Tony: Yeah. A priest . . . called Friedman! Oy vey Maria! (**FATHER** and **SON** *have hysterics. Out of which . . .*)

Tom: Why did you never . . . you know?

Tony: Me?

Tom: Yeah.

Tony: Don't know really. It just never made much sense to me. And you know I'm just an old lefty at heart. I approve of the values, some of them, the compassion, but on the whole I see more evidence for its lack and I don't really approve of the structure and . . . you know, I'm too petty and schoolboy to resist the wind-up. The only religion I really enjoy is Hinduism and that's purely because it annoys religious Jews so much because it's just so much older than anything else. They hate that. And I love it that they hate it. Sad but true. Keeps me going. And there's other things too like the Hindu stories are more colourful and it's got no founder and there are lots of Gods to choose from and it kind of admits that it's a messy indefinable thing and of course I couldn't do it because apart from anything I'd miss the beef! But don't get me wrong, all that's positive and bollocks, I like it best because it pisses off the Orthodox. And Christianity is tricky— and I'm very proud of you and all that—and I don't think you're turning on the gas or anything. I mean I hope you know that, and I can see it makes you happy and that's more or less good enough for me, but Christianity you know . . . Tricky, and not just because of the historical example it has set in its relation to power—barbaric! And it's fine now and everything because the church has no teeth and that's exactly the way it should be if you ask me, but it's because of sin and punishment and is it really very human to believe in everlasting punishment and I don't know but, and I'm sorry for being all Jewish all of a sudden but it's because at some point it, y'know all this, son, Christianity does become personal to Jews because eventually it's the Jews who get the blame for bungling the initial you know, the thing.

Tom: The Crucifixion?

Tony: Yeah. Exactly. So there you go. That's me. Tony Friedman on religion. I'm starving where's our food?

Tom: I just really want Mum to understand, that's all.

Tony: She might not, son.

Tom: I know . . .

Tony: Just give her some time to get used to the idea.

Tom: Yeah.

Tony: Yeah. I like Ruth. I really do. She *scares* me a little. Smashing girl.

Tom: Dad!

Tony: Yeah. Smashing. How is she?

Tom: Loves being pregnant.

Tony: Your mother was the same. Bloody hell. Women. How do they survive their bodies?

Tom: I'm going to ask her to marry me.

Tony: Good.

Tom: You think?

Tony: Absolutely. Though if your mother was here she'd want me to make sure you're doing the right thing.

Tom: It's a bit late for that isn't it?

Tony: Yeah but no harm in thinking. Pass me that napkin.

MASS APPEAL

BY BILL C. DAVIS

The issue in this scene is church reform in Catholicism. MARK, *the young seminarian, is a firebrand eager to drag the Church into the twenty-first century while* HIS *mentor,* FATHER TIM FARLEY, *tries to explain the need to move slowly and conservatively.* MARK *has been serving as a deacon in* FATHER FARLEY's *parish for some months and has just delivered a radical sermon calling for the Church "to become obsolete" when its spiritual goals are achieved. The scene begins with* FATHER FARLEY *speaking on the phone to a parishioner, while patiently explaining to* MARK *the error of* HIS *approach. The discussion quickly grows more serious, however, as the two wrestle over deeper issues of church politics, clerical celibacy, and* MARK's *vocation.*

FATHER FARLEY: Yes—well, he's very young and high-spirited—like a thoroughbred at the starting gate . . . I know you come to Mass because of me, Helen, but he has to start somewhere. I mean, if he were going to be a dentist, there would have to be that first set of molars. . . . I— (*House phone buzzes.*) Listen—I have to run, Helen. Oh—and thanks again for the "bubbly" and will you thank Jim for me too—will you? . . . Yes—don't worry. I'll be speaking to him very soon. You bet. Thanks for calling, Helen. (HE *presses the intercom button.*) Yes, Margaret. . . . Oh—he is. Good. Send him in. (FATHER FARLEY *pours himself a glass* *of wine—*MARK *enters dressed in* HIS *deacon's suit.*) Well, Mark—the parish poll is in and eighty percent of those interviewed, after having seen the spirit move you, feel that you and the spirit should move each other to the rustic bakery in the mountains with the Trappists. But take heart. You might be able to convince the Trappists to expand the bakery—that way you can have jelly doughnuts every day.

MARK: Why did you invite the faculty?

FATHER FARLEY: I didn't invite them. They come, like everyone else, to hear me. And they were surprised and thrilled to hear from you that the purpose of the church is to become obsolete.

MARK: The faculty shouldn't matter. You said that the people decide.

FATHER FARLEY: They do.

MARK: Well—they stopped coughing.

FATHER FARLEY: They also stopped breathing. (*Phone buzzes.* FATHER FARLEY *answers.*) Yes, Margaret. . . . Tell him I'm out. . . . Margaret—this is no time for scruples. I can't deal with Mr. Hartigan now. . . . What? . . . All right, Margaret. . . . All right, all right—then let me get to him before he gets angry for being kept waiting. (*Presses phone button.*) Hello, Mr. Hartigan. . . . Oh you were. . . . Yes—he's a deacon. . . . Yes—well—he's very young and high spirited; like a thoroughbred at the starting gate. . . . I know the church is not a race-track, Mr. Hartigan. . . . I'm sorry he made you uncomfortable. . . . I know you worked hard for everything you own. I don't think he was denying that. . . . I agree—there's no need for you to feel shackled. . . . Pardon me? . . . Yes—I got the bottle of sparkling burgundy you and Mrs. Hartigan sent me. Thank you and thank her for me too, will you? . . . No—not at all. I'm glad you called. It's always good to know the pulse of the parish. Goodbye Mr. Hartigan. (He *hangs up.* He *avoids looking at* Mark *as* Mark *moves toward* Him.)

Mark: Why do you let them do that to you?

Father Farley: Mark—when I first came here, the people didn't want me. The priest I replaced was well loved and no one was happy about his transfer. I was compared to him—the men ignored me—the women were painfully polite. Rich men in their sick beds chastised me for not coming to visit them sooner. I would come home to my room after my daily rounds and either throw something or burst into tears. I'd get to bed by eleven o'clock and maybe fall asleep by four a.m. I broke out in a rash all over my body except my face and my hands. And whatever kept that rash off my hands and face got me through. I have now achieved a level of beloved. A level I have basked in for the last ten years and for which I have never had to fight as hard as I had to this morning. Now would you please tell me what happened to you in that pulpit?

Mark: I gave my alternate sermon.

Father Farley: You lost control!

Mark: Yes—I lost control and I'm glad I did.

Father Farley: A priest should inspire control.

Mark: This morning I felt like a priest for the first time.

Father Farley: I don't want to hear about "the spirit moving you."

Mark: I can't explain it any other way. Why does it have to be explained?

FATHER FARLEY: Because nobody's buying that you're a thorough-bred at the starting gate.

MARK: Then don't try to sell them that. It was a mystery to me, let it be a mystery to them. Not everything can be explained, for God's sake. The core of the church is extra-scientific and unexplainable.

FATHER FARLEY: Mark—my congregation is not some primitive tribe who'll watch in awe as their priest becomes possessed by some preternatural force. You can't go on a rampage like that and expect to be understood. I've never had so many phone calls—never. And the collection went down thirty percent. It's no accident that the collection comes after the sermon. It's like the Nielsen rating.

MARK: (*Pause.*) Father—if I'm making things difficult for you here, I'll speak to Monsignor Burke and ask him to let you off the hook, and I'll go back to the seminary. (*Silence.*) . . . .

FATHER FARLEY: (*Phone buzzes.* **FATHER FARLEY** *answers.*) Yes, Margaret. . . . Oh, no. . . . How does he sound? . . . Oh for. . . . Okay—thank you, Margaret. (*Presses the hold button.*) Mark—could you excuse me for a minute. This is private.

MARK: Should I leave for the day?

FATHER FARLEY: No—Margaret's doing some work in the kitchen—she'd love the company. I won't be long. (**MARK** *exits.* **FATHER FARLEY** *presses outside line.*) Hello, Tom! Glad you called. I was just thinking about you. We never did get a chance to look at those pictures from Barcelona. . . . Could you get a hold of your sister. . . . Saturday sounds great. . . . All right see you then, Tom. . . . Pardon me? Yes—Mark Dolson did give a sermon. I would have invited you but. . . . Yes—I think he did say something about the purpose of the church is to become obsolete, but I'm sure he meant it as a joke. . . . No—nobody laughed. . . . Now Tom—I'm sure all of our jobs are safe for at least another five hundred years. . . . It only "sounded" radical. . . . Tom— the fact is Mark didn't say anything he didn't have a right to say. Even the faculty said that. . . . Yes—I'll send him over to you, but you don't have to talk to him about the sermon. I've already showed him what he did wrong. . . . It's not? . . . What do you want to see him about? . . . I see. . . . But he's always alone. . . . I think he defended them because he felt they had a right to change. I really don't think it was anything more than that. . . . Yes—I know you like to be sure. . . . Yes—I'll get him over to you. . . . What? . . . Oh—right—yes—see you Saturday, Tom. (**He** *hangs up.* **He** *calls offstage.*) Mark! Can you come in here, please.

MARK: (*From offstage.*) I'm helping Margaret with the dishes.

FATHER FARLEY: (*Calling out.*) Never mind about the dishes. Get in here now! (**MARK** *enters, sleeves rolled up, carrying a dish towel.*)

MARK: I just have a few more pots.

FATHER FARLEY: Monsignor Burke wants to see you right after you finish here.

MARK: He's upset about the sermon.

FATHER FARLEY: He says it's not about the sermon.

MARK: It's not?

FATHER FARLEY: Monsignor feels . . . and is afraid that you were too . . . vehement in your defense of Frank Kearney and Alfred Virasi. And he wants to talk to you about a possible connection.

MARK: He's nuts!

FATHER FARLEY: That's just the kind of intelligent approach he's hoping you'll resort to.

MARK: Do I have to put up with this? Can't I see the bishop?

FATHER FARLEY: The bishop is so paranoid about everything that's happened he wishes all the altar boys were girls. The bishop will let Burke do what he wants.

MARK: What do you think he's going to ask me?

FATHER FARLEY: It's hard to say. These interviews change according to the person he's inter—. . . . Let's do it.

MARK: What?

FATHER FARLEY: The interview. I'll play Monsignor Burke and you play you.

MARK: I shouldn't have to go through with this—at all.

FATHER FARLEY: Mark—relax. You don't have anything to be afraid of, do you? Come on—just go out and come in like you're coming in for the interview.

MARK: I don't want to play a psycho game.

FATHER FARLEY: Mark—you have to go through this with as much grace and tact as you can. You can't afford a repeat of your last encounter with him. (**MARK** *hesitates.*) Come on—stop wasting time. I have to get ready for my five-twenty Mass.

MARK: All right. (**MARK** *goes off and re-enters as if coming in for* **HIS** *interview with* **MONSIGNOR BURKE**.)

FATHER FARLEY: (*As* **BURKE**.) Good day, Dolson. (**MARK** *laughs at the apparent accuracy of the impersonation.*)

MARK: Hello, Monsignor Burke.

FATHER FARLEY: (*As* **MONSIGNOR BURKE.**) You're late.

MARK: I am? Well . . . I've been fasting all week and meditating every night so time and space are. . . .

FATHER FARLEY: (*As* **MONSIGNOR BURKE.**) That's very interesting, Dolson. Tell me—have you considered a career in a contemplative order?

MARK: Funny you should say that. Father Farley was suggesting that very thing to me just today.

FATHER FARLEY: (*As* **MONSIGNOR BURKE.**) Well—he manages to come up with a few good ideas every. . . . (As himself.) Leave me out of this. (*As* **MONSIGNOR BURKE.**) Now—I'd like to ask you a few questions. My first question has to do with Frank Kearney and Alfred Virasi.

MARK: No—he wouldn't get into that right away.

FATHER FARLEY: He's a busy man.

MARK: If he's so busy he can skip my interview.

FATHER FARLEY: All right—have it your way. (*As* **MONSIGNOR BURKE.**) How's your family?

MARK: Fine. Thank you.

FATHER FARLEY: (*As* **MONSIGNOR BURKE.**) There's one thing I've always been curious about in regards to your family life, Dolson. Why did you leave home at sixteen?

MARK: I wanted to be on my own.

FATHER FARLEY: (*As* **MONSIGNOR BURKE.**) But so young. Was there something at home pushing you out?

MARK: I don't think I realized it at the time but there was a silence in my house that . . . crushed me. There were choruses going on inside of me and at dinner we all chewed and clanked and there were times I felt the fork would melt right in my hand.

FATHER FARLEY: So you left.

MARK: Yes.

FATHER FARLEY: Where did you go?

MARK: (*Pause.*) What were you asking about Frank and Alfred?

FATHER FARLEY: (*As* MONSIGNOR BURKE.) Well—I have been wondering why you reacted so strongly to my suggestion that they take off a year from their studies.

MARK: It was not a suggestion—it was a demand. They did not take a year off—you kicked them out.

FATHER FARLEY: (*As* MONSIGNOR BURKE.) All right. If you want to be direct. Do you think priests should be allowed to sleep together?

MARK: They weren't priests—they weren't even deacons. A vow of celibacy was far off for them.

FATHER FARLEY: (*As* MONSIGNOR BURKE.) Do you think such practices are easily dispensed with?

MARK: (*Amused.*) Practices? Would you care to be more specific, Monsignor?

FATHER FARLEY: (*As* MONSIGNOR BURKE.) Just answer my question. (*As himself.*) Just answer his question.

MARK: Is your question something along the lines of—"How you gonna keep 'em down on the farm after they've seen Paree?"

FATHER FARLEY: (*As* **MONSIGNOR BURKE**.) Stop your verbal acrobatics and give a response to whatever you interpret my question to be.

MARK: Yes! I think Frank and Alfred would have stayed down on the farm after they had seen Paree.

FATHER FARLEY: (*As* **MONSIGNOR BURKE**.) Let me ask my next question in your native tongue. Have you ever seen Paree? And if you have seen Paree—were they Parisiettes—or Parisians?

MARK: (*Long pause.*) Both.

FATHER FARLEY: Really?

MARK: That's it! No more. You were shocked.

FATHER FARLEY: I was playing Monsignor Burke.

MARK: No—that was. . . .

FATHER FARLEY: Both?

MARK: Yes! Women and men—two sexes. Monsignor—before I came to the seminary I enrolled myself in a three-year orgy that laid waste to every fibre of my character. Does that sound apologetic enough? How about this? Monsignor Burke—please understand—I explored the world by indulging my sexual ambivalence. I searched, with my body, and I discovered that I could never reconcile my inner emotional world that way. Others have—but my unique, personal and human condition called for another way. So . . . I invite celibacy—I will be happy to stay down on the farm because it's there I will be calm enough to help others and the only real joy in this world is helping other people. I feel determined and perfectly prepared to become a priest. (*Pause.*) What would he say to that?

FATHER FARLEY: Both?

MARK: Will you stop?

FATHER FARLEY: I'm sorry—It's just . . . I've never seen you in this light before.

MARK: What light?

FATHER FARLEY: Red light.

MARK: And you've never been in "red light"?

FATHER FARLEY: By the time my father left and my mother died, I was so confused I didn't want to be near man, woman, or piano leg. Celibacy came naturally to me. Mark, if Monsignor Burke asks you, say—"Yes—I did make love with Parisiettes."

MARK: That's a half-truth.

FATHER FARLEY: Don't start throwing principles around now, Mark. This is too serious for principles. In the larger scheme of things, Monsignor Burke is not that important.

MARK: But the truth is that I won't become a priest on a lie.

FATHER FARLEY: Better that than none at all.

MARK: I can't believe you're saying this. I won't listen. (**MARK** *starts to go*.)

FATHER FARLEY: Fine—don't listen to me. Go over there and do your martyr number. Just leave your forwarding address behind. (**MARK** *turns and goes to* **FATHER FARLEY**.)

MARK: He can't get rid of me.

FATHER FARLEY: He can get rid of you. (*Pause.*) Mark—once you're a priest you can fight him all you want. Just make sure you do become a priest. Try it my way. Be diplomatic. Avoid answering questions directly. You can steer the questions. Phrase your answers certain ways. . . .

MARK: You mean lie.

FATHER FARLEY: Even Christ said to his disciples, be as innocent as doves and as cunning as serpents. Christ said that.

MARK: Does cunning mean lying?

FATHER FARLEY: If you can afford not to be a priest—tell the truth. If you want to be a priest—lie. (*Silence—*MARK *is on the verge of tears.*) Mark—I want you to become a priest. I asked for you.

MARK: You asked for me? You told me. . . .

FATHER FARLEY: I know. I told you Monsignor Burke made me do this—that he forced this special assignment on me. He didn't. I asked him to let me help you.

MARK: Why?

FATHER FARLEY: Because you're a lunatic! And the church needs lunatics—you're one of those priceless lunatics that comes along every so often and makes the church alive. The only problem with lunatics is they don't know how to survive. I do. (*Pause.* FATHER FARLEY *holds out* HIS *keys to* HIS *Mercedes.*) Here—take my car. (MARK *looks at the keys. After a pause* HE *takes them and exits as lights fade to black.*)

NEXT FALL
BY GEOFFREY NAUFFTS

LUKE *and* ADAM *are lovers, and the scene takes place "the morning after the night before." Both suddenly realize that* LUKE*'s religious faith will soon come into conflict with* ADAM*'s atheism. The playwright builds a breezy, chatty, and honest dialogue between these partners that easily introduces* THEM *in* THEIR *first encounter to the religious divide that separates* THEM*. On one level, the scene reads like a typical modern sitcom, but on another, much deeper level, it raises questions that won't easily disappear once the scene is over. The two actors should strive to capture the rising tension in the scene, and the deep conflict between* LUKE *and* ADAM *that emerges only at the end.*

LUKE: Wait'll you taste these tomatoes. They're fierce.

ADAM: (*Offstage.*) Fierce? Tomatoes aren't fierce. Lions are. Madonna is. Tomatoes are just . . . tomatoes.

LUKE: Where you been, Grandpa? Madonna hasn't been fierce since she was a virgin. (ADAM *enters in* HIS *boxers with a big smile on* HIS *face.*)

ADAM: I know I said it already, but you were really amazing last night.

LUKE: You mean it?

ADAM: When you told me you were the Stage Manager, I didn't realize it was an actual part.

LUKE: The lead part.

ADAM: You were brilliant. The whole production was. I cried.

LUKE: I know, I heard you. . . . Everyone in the audience heard you.

ADAM: I'm having a mid-life crisis. It was cathartic. (**ADAM** *sits in front of a plate of eggs.*) Looks. Delicious.

LUKE: It's the best I could do with what you had in your fridge.

ADAM: I didn't even know I had a fridge.

LUKE: Dig in before it gets cold.

ADAM: I think the only one who cried more than me was that weird lady in the turban.

LUKE: That was my mother.

ADAM: Did I say weird? I meant eccentric.

LUKE: Turbans are her thing right now. Last year it was tracksuits. The year before it was chunky jewelry. (**ADAM** *starts eating.*)

ADAM: And your dad?

LUKE: He was a no-show. Still mad I dropped out of law school, I guess. It's just as well. He gets kind of cranky whenever he and my mom are in the same room together. The "Arlene Show" can be a little exhausting after twenty years.

ADAM: How long have they been divorced?

LUKE: Twenty years. He kind of turned his life around after they split up. It was just me and him for a while there. I was like his little security blanket. He dragged me everywhere.

ADAM: So, that must have been challenging. Your folks divorcing when you were so young.

LUKE: I was just glad the craziness was over.

ADAM: What kind of crazy?

LUKE: Like waking up in the middle of the night to a house full of pot smoke. Pink Floyd on the stereo, the front door wide open and nobody in sight.

ADAM: Sounds like my entire four years of college.

LUKE: Well, it's no fun when you're in kindergarten, trust me. To this day, the smell of patchouli oil makes me weep. (ADAM *watches, curiously, as* LUKE *closes* HIS *eyes for a moment, prays, then opens them again and digs in.*)

ADAM: What was that?

LUKE: What was what?

ADAM: Where'd you go just then?

LUKE: I was praying.

ADAM: You mean, crystals and chakras? Like a Deepak Chopra kind of thing?

LUKE: Not really.

ADAM: Then, who were you praying to?

LUKE: God.

ADAM: Oh. (*The honeymoon just ended.*)

LUKE: Yum.

ADAM: Is that an everyday occurrence?

Luke: Pretty much.

Adam: So, you're what, then. . . . You're—a . . .

Luke: Christian.

Adam: Okay. (**Adam** *tries to proceed with* **His** *breakfast as usual.*)

Luke: Does that freak you out?

Adam: Does it freak me out?

Luke: Yeah.

Adam: Why would it freak me out?

Luke: No reason. . . . Why? What are you?

Adam: What am I?

Luke: Besides a vamper.

Adam: Nothing . . . I don't know. I didn't really grow up with a religion. (**Luke** *stabs a tomato and pops it into* **His** *mouth.*)

Luke: These tomatoes are fierce. I don't care what you say. (**Adam** *looks at* **Him***, suspiciously.*)

Adam: You're gay though, right?

Luke: Uh . . . whose lips do you think you were mackin' on all night?

Adam: I know, but don't Catholics consider that a sin?

Luke: Uh-huh.

Adam: So, how does that work, then?

Luke: How does what work?

Adam: Being gay and . . . you know. . . .

LUKE: This is gonna be a problem, isn't it?

ADAM: No . . . I'm . . . I just . . .

LUKE: We're all sinners, Adam. We all struggle with one thing or another. This one just happens to be mine.

ADAM: Do you atone, then? Is that what you do?

LUKE: You really want to talk about this?

ADAM: Sure. (**LUKE** *indulges* **HIM**.)

LUKE: You accept Christ as the Son of God. That He died on the cross for all your sins.

ADAM: That's it?

LUKE: Pretty much.

ADAM: And you'll go to heaven?

LUKE: If you believe. If you truly believe.

ADAM: And you do.

LUKE: Uh-huh. (**LUKE** *refills* **ADAM**'s *coffee*.)

ADAM: Then how come you continue to sin? I mean, and don't get me wrong, that was some amazing sinning we just did, I look forward to more, but you sinned a lot. You sinned more than I did.

LUKE: I was hoping we could sin again after breakfast.

ADAM: You didn't answer my question.

LUKE: It's human nature, Adam. We can't escape it. But as long as you've accepted Christ. . . . (*A beat.*)

ADAM: Is that why you didn't introduce me to your mom last night?

Luke: I didn't?

Adam: Nope.

Luke: Might have had a little something to do with it. (**Luke** *rises and starts clearing the table.*)

Adam: So, let me see if I got this right. I'm assuming sin is sin. And if your sin is having sex with men, and my sin is, say, *killing* men who have sex with men, then as long as I've accepted Christ as my Savior, I'll go to heaven with you?

Luke: Killing men who have sex with men? You mean, like Jeffrey Dahmer?

Adam: Yeah . . . well, no. Because he killed them, then he ate them. Plus, he had sex with them too, so no, not him.

Luke: Like who, then?

Adam: The guys who killed Matthew Shepard. (*A beat.*)

Luke: Technically, yes.

Adam: Not only that, but I can continue to kill men who have sex with men, much as you continue to have sex with them, every day for the rest of my life, and still go to heaven?

Luke: Well. . . .

Adam: It's just a hypothesis.

Luke: I know it sounds terrible, but . . . yes.

Adam: Huh. (*Can't quite let it go.*) So, then, if Matthew Shepard hadn't accepted Christ before he died, he's in hell, and his killers who, say, have, are going to heaven? Is that what you're saying? (**Luke** *stands there with* **His** *arms full.*)

Luke: Can we change the subject?

TURTLE ISLAND BLUES
BY WILLIAM BORDEN

One of the most perverse historical crimes committed by Western colonists against tribal peoples was (and still is) the attempt to stamp out native culture and beliefs by forcibly converting indigenous inhabitants to Christianity. Under the guise of bringing salvation to the heathen, many well-meaning missionaries participated in this effort in North America, spearheading exploration and eventually leading to the establishment of the notorious system of "Indian schools." In this hilarious scene, the missionary VICKERY *(playing the role of the historical Father Jan de Smet), attempts to explain fundamental concepts of the Christian faith to* SITTING BULL.

FATHER VICKERY: Sitting Bull, I'm Father De Smet. I'd like to give you this cross—it's big medicine—and I'd like you to consider becoming a Christian.

SITTING BULL: Why?

FATHER VICKERY: Well, for one, thing, it'll help you live a moral life. For example, now, when you get the urge to—you know. . . .

SITTING BULL: Oh, I do that only with my wife.

FATHER VICKERY: But don't you get the urge to—you know—wander?

Sitting Bull: Oh, sure.

Father Vickery: What do you do then?

Sitting Bull: Have lots of wives.

Father Vickery: That's immoral.

Sitting Bull: We don't have any illegitimate children.

Father Vickery: Illegitimate children are a sign of civilization. Accept this cross, Sitting Bull. It's the one true faith.

Sitting Bull: Which Christian faith is it now that's the one true one? I hear the same thing from the Lutherans, the Mormons, the Baptists—

Father Vickery: The important thing is that it's Christian.

Sitting Bull: But I don't feel a need for anything like that, Father.

Father Vickery: Ah! There you are! What is it we all need?

Sitting Bull: Food. They said if we came in to the reservations, we'd get rations. The government killed all the buffalo, the settlers killed all the game. They promised us cattle, flour—but we haven't gotten anything. And those little biscuits you hand out, Father, that's not enough to feed us.

Father Vickery: Those little biscuits are the body of Christ.

Sitting Bull: That's his body?

Father Vickery: And the wine is his blood.

Sitting Bull: And Christ's been dead two thousand years?

Father Vickery: It's a miracle, isn't it?

SITTING BULL: Let me see if I've got this right, Father. Once upon a time the Great Spirit decided to become a man. He decided to become a man, even though he knew he was going to be killed. He let himself be killed so he could become the Great Spirit again. He did all that so people could live forever. But to live forever they have to believe this cockamamie story. Why didn't he just tell people they could live forever in the first place?

FATHER VICKERY: These are very complicated theological matters, Sitting Bull.

SITTING BULL: And now, every time you say "Hocus pocus," that biscuit turns into his body and that wine turns into his blood, and you eat his body and drink his blood, but the biscuit still tastes like a biscuit and the wine still tastes like wine. And this dead man wants you to eat him every week. Do I have this right?

FATHER VICKERY: Well—

SITTING BULL: That's disgusting.

FATHER VICKERY: You're not looking at this in the proper frame of mind.

SITTING BULL: I guess I'm just a superstitious savage. I believe that all life is sacred. I believe that the earth is my mother. Father, I'm just not sophisticated enough to be a Christian.

DOG SEES GOD: CONFESSIONS OF A TEENAGE BLOCKHEAD
BY BERT V. ROYAL

CB and Van *are high school buddies, and* CB *has been dating* Van*'s sister, who is now in rehab for starting fires.* CB*'s dog has recently died, which has forced* Him *to think about the "metaphysical" subject of death. In this scene, the two turn over some ideas on that subject.* CB *and* Van *sit on the remnant of a brick wall.* Van *is smoking a joint. He offers it to* CB.

Van: You wanna hit this?

CB: No. Thanks.

Van: (*Smiling.*) It's kind bud. You sure, man?

CB: Nah, I'm good.

Van: I've been meaning to tell you—I'm sorry about your dog.

CB: Thanks, man.

Van: He was a good dog.

CB: Yeah. He was.

Van: But he was old. It was long past his time. Still—he was a good dog. I totally wanted to come to your funeral party thingy, but I was waiting on a delivery from the Doober.

CB: What do you think happens when we die?

VAN: Do you mean, like, do I believe in heaven?

CB: Yeah.

VAN: Nah, man. I'm a Buddhist.

CB: Since when?

VAN: It's kind of a new development.

CB: Well, what do Buddhists believe happens when you die?

VAN: Buddha believed that one of two things happens. Either you are reborn or you dissolve into nothingness. Oddly enough, the former is punishment and the latter, reward. We Buddhists believe that the corporeal body is the source of all suffering and a liberation from the body into nothingness, or nirvana, is the fuckin' way to go.

CB: Don't you find that depressing?

VAN: Liberation?

CB: Nothingness.

VAN: I think I'd kind of like to be nothingness. Because even nothing is something, right? (**He** *shows* **His** *hand to* **CB**.) What am I holding in my hand?

CB: Nothing.

VAN: One would say that, yes. But in that nothingness is a thousand things, right? Particles and atoms and tens of thousands of things that we might not even know about yet. I could be holding in my hand the secrets of the universe and the answers to everything.

CB: You're stoned.

Van: Damn straight. (**CB** *laughs*.) Why this interest in the afterlife? Is this about your dog?

CB: Just curious.

Van: Dude, we all have to let go of things from our childhood. Do you remember when you and my sister burned my blanket to teach me that?

CB: Yeah. It was only two months ago. If I'd known that it would lead to her being—well—I wouldn't have let her do it.

Van: I was so pissed at you guys.

CB: The thing was fuckin' nasty, man.

Van: (*Pissed.*) Still. Y'all suck.

CB: I think you were about to make a point.

Van: I was?

CB: Never mind. I think I got it.

Van: My point is, Chuck B., that life—it does go on. Even without the things that have been there since the beginning. The things that we think define us, don't mean shit in the grand scheme of things. Us defines us. Not things or other people or pets. Like, me without my blanket—it's still me. I miss my fuckin' blanket, though. That was a dick thing y'all did.

CB: Three words for you, bro—(One finger.) Pubic. (*Two fingers.*) Lice. (*Three fingers.*) Infestation.

Van: Could've been fixed.

CB: Hey, we let you keep the ashes.

Van: I smoked 'em.

CB: You what?

Van: I rolled 'em with some good herb and smoked that shit up.

CB: That's sick.

Van: Now, my blanket and I are like one forever.

CB: That's seriously disturbed, dawg.

Van: We all handle grief in different ways.

CB: Can't be good for you.

Van: Dude! Showed you two! Tryin' to mess with my shit. HA!

CB: Hey, how is your sister doing?

Van: She's good. The doctors say that she's getting better. (*Pause.*) Damn, I miss that bitch.

CB: So do I.

Van: This conversation is a major downer, amigo. Dead dogs, missing sisters, burning blankets. Let's talk about something happy.

CB: Like what? (**They** *sit in silence, the light fades slowly out.*)

TIES THAT BIND: FEATURING THE ASTOUNDING KRISPINSKY

BY ERIC COBLE

"Everyman" is the subject of this satirical monologue/duologue that describes the condensed life-to-death history of KRISPINSKY *in three short minutes.* MARCO, *the narrator, speaks directly to the audience as a vaudeville "barker," while the second actor hilariously mimes the behavior that* MARCO *describes. Among other issues, the monologue raises the question of God's problematic place in this divine comedy.*

MARCO: Ladies and gentlemen, if you are on good terms with any deity of any consequence whatsoever—call in that favor now. Get praying. We have defibrillators and clean undergarments at the rear of the house for those in need. For tonight you are about to witness a feat of such cunning, such bravado, such gut-churning moxie that it will only—can only—be attempted by one man. And that one man . . . is none other . . . than the astounding Krispinsky!!

(*Wild applause.* KRISPINSKY *is carried in—stiff, horizontal, hands behind* HIS *back, seemingly bound by invisible means—by two stagehands.* HE *is laid on the floor.* HE *nods to the audience as the stagehands leave.* HE *is earnest.*)

Ladies and gentlemen, the man you see helpless before you has cheated death a thousand times in a thousand ways. Why, on this very stage, scarcely eighteen months ago, you saw this hero emerge from a sealed tank of flesh-rending piranha wearing nothing but the loincloth given him for luck by his dying syphilitic grandmother. But tonight he will undergo the Greatest—perhaps the Final—Challenge Of His Life. Can we have the clock?

(*A clock appears, set to count down from three minutes.*)

He will have three minutes. One hundred eighty seconds. Are you ready, Krispinsky? (**KRISPINSKY** nods.) Are your nerves steeled? (**KRISPINSKY** nods.) Then . . . prepare . . . to escape . . . from your own Life! GO!

(*The clock starts ticking down. . . .* **KRISPINSKY** *starts wriggling, trying to get* **HIS** *hands around* **HIS** *legs in front of* **HIM**.)

He's off! He's grappling with Parental Approval! Vying for his parents' affection against three other siblings—trying out for basketball, singing operettas at family Christmas parties—but . . . NO!

(**KRISPINSKY** *writhes.*)

He's snagged by his parents' Distant Lack of Attention! His father's more interested in the sports page than his own son's minor concussion! A mother who needs a fully stocked pharmacy to get dinner on the table every night—

(**KRISPINSKY** *gets* **HIS** *hands in front of* **HIM**—*struggles to stand . . .*)

But by sheer force of hormonal rebellion he's on his feet!

(**KRISPINSKY** *keeps twisting—trying to get* **HIS** *feet separated to maintain* **HIS** *balance.*)

But he's still got to get through his Hyper-Consciousness of His Physical Appearance—the left ear slightly smaller than the right, the gangly arms—the ACNE—oh God, he's almost free of the acne—

(**Krispinsky** *gets* **His** *feet spread.*)

He's functioning—

(**Krispinsky** *tries to open* **His** *mouth with* **His** *bound hands.*)

—but there's his inability to Communicate with the Opposite Sex! With only his parents' failed marriage and a handful of teen romance movies as guides—can he use his out-sized bravado to mask his stunted inner life? He's doing it . . .

(**Krispinsky** *smashes to the ground.*)

NOOOO! Student loans!! Can even the mightiest among us claw through a solid mountain of debt?? He's trying—money management books, a seminar—

(**Krispinsky** *writhes—arching* **His** *body to get up . . .*)

He's got automatic payroll deduction—He's Standing!

(**Krispinsky**'s *legs are knocked out from under* **Him.**)

He's Down! Blind-sided by Internalized Religious Convictions! If it feels good, it must be wrong—what if someone finds those magazines and videos under the bed??

(**Krispinsky**'s *right arms shoots out—free.*)

An arm free! Moving out into the world—

(**Krispinsky** *begins jerking back and forth—back and forth . . .*)

Get Married! Stay Single! Get Married! Stay Single!

(**Krispinsky** *falls to* **His** *knees—struggling . . .*)

Get Married! Have Children!

(**He** *sinks lower . . .*)

House Payments!

(*Lower.*)

Lawn needs to be mowed, tub re-grouted. Ikea furniture assembled—Can he do it??

(**Krispinsky**'s *other arm shoots free—*)

He's almost there!!

(**Krispinsky** *tries to stand . . . a tremendous force on* **His** *back—* **He** *falls—*)

Oh! Inability to Please! His Father rears its ugly head out of nowhere! His own parenting skills questioned—the parent-teacher conferences he's missed—not helping with the Cub Scout Pinewood Derby—He's become his own father!

(**Krispinsky** *turns in on himself . . . hopping . . .*)

He's taking care of his own father! Find the right Nursing Home, the right Hospice, the right Crematorium—Almost free . . .

(**Krispinsky** *is almost up . . .*)

But empty! Sleepless nights—"is this all there is?" Forty years of work and life and work—for what? Paging Jean Paul Sartre! Paging Jean Paul Sartre!

(**Krispinsky** *is up . . .*)

But he's . . . he's . . . he's a Free Man!!

(**KRISPINSKY** *arches back—arms out—legs spread—triumphant—FREE! The clock hits zero—Wild applause.*)

KRISPINSKY: AAAAAAHHHH!!—

(**HIS** *eyes go wide,* **HIS** *jaw drops . . .* **HE** *tumbles backward. Lies still on the ground.*)

MARCO: And he's Dead!! Oh! Ladies and gentlemen, the astounding Krispinsky finds true freedom at last! Give it up for the Ultimate Escape!

(**MARCO** *leads applause as the two stagehands run on and carry the dead* **KRISPINSKY** *offstage.*)

FAMILY DEVOTIONS
BY DAVID HENRY HWANG

DI-GOU *is visiting* HIS *wealthy relations in the States, now that* HIS *wife has passed away;* HIS *two sisters migrated from China thirty years ago, and* HE *has never met* HIS *niece Jenny, or* HIS *nephew Chester, who is greatly relieved to be getting out of the house and launching* HIS *career as a violinist with the Boston Symphony. During* HIS *visit* DI-GOU *struggles to catch-up with all the changes that have occurred in* HIS *siblings since they migrated from China.* HE *believes that family ties and ancestors are more important than culture or religion, but* HIS *sisters have clung to a version of Christianity instilled in them years ago by their mother, a fervent Chinese evangelist, See-goh-poh. As the scene opens,* DI-GOU *is sitting alone on the tennis court after a new American-made ball-serving tennis machine has run amok. Suddenly,* HE'*s hit by a tennis ball playfully thrown by* HIS *nephew* CHESTER, *who enters, carrying a violin case.*

CHESTER: Quite a workout, there.

DI-GOU: America is full of surprises—why do all these products function so poorly?

CHESTER: Looks like "Made in the US" is gonna become synonymous with defective workmanship. (*Pause.*) You wanna see my violin?

DI-GOU: I would love to.

CHESTER: I thought you might. Here. (**HE** *removes the violin from the case*.) See? No "Made in US" label.

DI-GOU: It is beautiful.

CHESTER: Careful! The back has a lacquer which never dries—so don't touch it, or you'll leave your fingerprints in it forever.

DI-GOU: Imagine that. After I die, someone could be playing a violin with my fingerprint.

CHESTER: Funny, isn't it?

DI-GOU: You know, I used to play violin.

CHESTER: Really?

DI-GOU: Though I never had so fine an instrument as this.

CHESTER: Try it, go ahead.

DI-GOU: No. Please. I get more pleasure looking at it than I would playing it. But I would get the most pleasure hearing you play.

CHESTER: No.

DI-GOU: Please?

CHESTER: All right. Later. How long did you play?

DI-GOU: Some years. During the Cultural Revolution, I put it down.

CHESTER: Must've been tough, huh? (**HE** *directs* **DI-GOU***'s attention to the back of* **HIS** *violin*.) Look—the back's my favorite part.

DI-GOU: China is my home, my work. I had to stay there. (**HE** *looks at the back of the violin*.) Oh—the way the light reflects—look. And I can see myself in it.

CHESTER: Yeah. Nice, huh?

DI-GOU: So you will take this violin and make music around the world.

CHESTER: Around the world? Oh, you probably got a misleading press clipping. See, my dad . . .

DI-GOU: Very funny.

CHESTER: (*Smiling.*) Yeah. See, I'm just playing in the Boston Symphony. I'm leaving tomorrow.

DI-GOU: I am fortunate, then, to come today, or perhaps I would never meet you.

CHESTER: You know, I wasn't even planning to come here.

DI-GOU: That would be terrible. You know, in China, my wife and I had no children—for the good of the state. (**HE** *moves to where* **HE** *left the Chinese toys earlier in the act.* **HE** *picks them up and studies them.*) All these years, I try to imagine—what does Hannah look like? What does her baby look like? Now, I finally visit and what do I find? A young man. A violinist. The baby has long since disappeared. And I learn I'll never know the answer to my question. (*Silence.*)

CHESTER: Di-Gou, why did you come here?

DI-GOU: My wife has died, I'm old. I've come for my sisters.

CHESTER: Well, I hope you're not disappointed to come here and see your sisters, your family, carry on like this.

DI-GOU: They are still my sisters.

CHESTER: I'm leaving here. Like you did.

DI-GOU: But, Chester, I've found that I cannot leave the family. Today—Look!—I follow them across an ocean.

CHESTER: You know, they're gonna start bringing you to church.

DI-GOU: No. My sisters and their religion are two different things.

CHESTER: No, they're not. You've been away. You've forgotten. This family breathes for God. Ever since your aunt, See-goh-poh.

DI-GOU: See-goh-poh is not the first member of this family.

CHESTER: She's the first Christian.

DI-GOU: There are faces further back than you can see. Faces long before the white missionaries arrived in China. Here. (**HE** *holds* **CHESTER***'s violin so that its back is facing* **CHESTER***, and uses it like a mirror.*) Look here. At your face. Study your face and you will see—the shape of your face is the shape of faces back many generations—across an ocean, in another soil. You must become one with your family before you can hope to live away from it.

CHESTER: Oh, sure, there're faces. But they don't matter here. See-goh-poh's face is the only one that has any meaning here.

DI-GOU: No. The stories written on your face are the ones you must believe.

CHESTER: Stories? I see stories, Di-Gou. All around me. This house tells a story. The days of the week tell a story—Sunday is a service, Wednesday and Friday are fellowship, Thursday is visitation. Even the furniture tells stories. Look around. See-goh-poh is sitting in every chair. There's nothing for me here.

DI-GOU: I am here.

CHESTER: You? All right. Here. (**HE** *turns the back of the violin toward* **DI-GOU***, again using it like a mirror.*) You look. You wanna know what I see? I see the shape of your face changing. And with it, a mind, a will, as different as the face. If you stay with them, your old self will go, and in its place will come a new man, an old man, a man who'll pray.

DI-GOU: Chester, you are in America. If you deny those who share your blood, what do you have in this country?

CHESTER: Your face is changing, Di-Gou. Before you know it, you'll be praying and speaking in tongues.

OUR LADY OF 121ST STREET

BY STEPHEN ADLY GUIRGIS

At first glance, there is little about ROOFTOP DESMOND *that suggests a man in need of spiritual help—yet here* HE *is, in* FATHER LUX's *confessional after many years on the street. Beneath the absurd comedy that peppers the dialogue in this scene, however, the playwright reveals a much more important issue: how Catholicism rises to the challenge of ministering to the needs of so many urban outcasts like* DESMOND. *In so doing, Stephen Adly Guirgis reminds us of the ancient wisdom: no matter what our station in life may be, "the poor you have always with you."*

ROOFTOP: Bless me Father for I have sinned . . . (*Pause.*) . . . a lot, know what I'm sayin' . . . ? Yes, sir . . . Um. . . . Are you, are you there, Father . . . ?

FATHER LUX: Yes.

ROOFTOP: Alright, jus' checkin'. . . . That you, Father Martin?

FATHER LUX: Uh, no.

ROOFTOP: Father Cunningham?

FATHER LUX: No.

ROOFTOP: Oh. . . . Where Father Cunningham at?

FATHER LUX: Excuse me?

ROOFTOP: I say, where Father Cunningham at?

FATHER LUX: Father Cunningham?

ROOFTOP: Yeah.

FATHER LUX: He's—no longer with us.

ROOFTOP: Father C—you talkin' 'bout?

FATHER LUX: Yes.

ROOFTOP: "No longer with us," huh?

FATHER LUX: Yes.

ROOFTOP: Father C?

FATHER LUX: Correct.

ROOFTOP: Dag . . . He didn't do something "bad," did he?

FATHER LUX: He's dead.

ROOFTOP: Dead?!

FATHER LUX: With God, yes.

ROOFTOP: Well, pardon me, but—why didn't you just say that then?

FATHER LUX: What?

ROOFTOP: I'm sayin', if the man's dead, juss say he dead.

FATHER LUX: I did.

ROOFTOP: Nah, you said "no longer with us"—like, like a "scandal" or something.

FATHER LUX: Are you here to make confession, sir?

ROOFTOP: Yes I am, but Father C was a close, personal friend of mine, and I can't really say I appreciate—

FATHER LUX: Father Cunningham has been dead for fifteen years, sir, OK? (*Pause.*)

ROOFTOP: Oh. . . . OK. . . . Sorry. . . .

FATHER LUX: So, how long since your last confession?

ROOFTOP: My last confession?

FATHER LUX: Yes.

ROOFTOP: The last one?

FATHER LUX: Yes.

ROOFTOP: You mean in a church?

FATHER LUX: In a church. Yes.

ROOFTOP: Right. Well . . . last one been . . . well . . . well, it's been . . . Know what I'm sayin'? It's been been. Definitely been been.

FATHER LUX: OK.

ROOFTOP: Put it like this: my first confession? That was the last time checkin' in with y'all, so, yeah, been a while . . . been . . . well—

FATHER LUX: Got it. Proceed.

ROOFTOP: 'Cuz I mean, ya know, my moms raised me right, went to school right upstairs, listened ta the nuns, Sister Rose and all, still . . . Shit! Is Father C really dead?

Father Lux: What?

Rooftop: 'Cuz I was hopin' ta get Father C.

Father Lux: Sir—

Rooftop: Guess everybody got ta go, right?

Father Lux: Yes.

Rooftop: Still, how's a man gonna up and die with no warning?

Father Lux: Sir—

Rooftop: Send a telegram, sumpthin': "Might die soon. FYI."

Father Lux: Perhaps you ought to collect yourself and come back later.

Rooftop: Hey Father, did you know that Father C one time got hit by a Mack truck but he was OK?

Father Lux: Sir—

Rooftop: See, us kids, we was playin' Booties Up on the wall across from here, but we was all standin' in the street like fools do, and—

Father Lux: Stop.

Rooftop: What, I can't relate a little anecdote?

Father Lux: What you can do, sir, is confess.

Rooftop: Confess, huh?

Father Lux: Confess your sins. Yes.

Rooftop: Dag, you all business, aint'cha, Father?

Father Lux: Sir—

Rooftop: No prelude nuthin'—just spit it out.

Father Lux: Sir—

Rooftop: "Early birds eat apples and worms"; I gotcha—got no argument wit' that.

Father Lux: OK then.

Rooftop: You got a forthright nature, Father—no nonsense—I respect that in a man.

Father Lux: Oh. Well—

Rooftop: Still, even Hank Aaron hit a few off the practice tee before he stepped up to the rock—gotta marinate before ya grill, right?

Father Lux: This is not a "cook-out," sir.

Rooftop: No, it's not—

Father Lux: No charcoal, no anecdotes, no franks and beans—

Rooftop: True 'dat—

Father Lux: This is, in fact, a confessional, sir. A confessional—not a "conversational"—do you understand that distinction?

Rooftop: I'll keep it moving.

Father Lux: Thank you.

Rooftop: OK . . . right. . . . So . . . so, yeah—I mean, whaddyacallit? The inter Venal Sins?

Father Lux: Venal.

Rooftop: What?

Father Lux: Venal.

ROOFTOP: Venal yeah—mucho venal. Venal sins, dass daily, daily occurrence. Prolly racked up a dozen since I walked up in here. . . . And, uh, Mortal Sin? Mortal Sins, Father? I mean, "pick a Commandment, any Commandment," know what I'm sayin'?

FATHER LUX: How 'bout you pick one?

ROOFTOP: Oh. . . . OK . . . uh. . . . Dag, Father, I'm juss . . . I'm juss a bad man, Father. Lyin', cheatin', stealin', and humpin'— Dag, Freebasing— . . . See, I'm the kind of a guy . . . one time I . . . well, there was this girl once . . . say Father, I can't smoke in here, right?

OUR LADY OF 121ST STREET

BY STEPHEN ADLY GUIRGIS

This scene follows later in the play, when FATHER LUX *seeks out* ROOFTOP, *whom* HE *finds hanging out with* HIS *street friends. This scene offers a remarkable "turnaround" toward the end, when* ROOFTOP *actually decides to join* FATHER LUX *in prayer.*

ROOFTOP: Aw, man, now what's all this about?

FATHER LUX: Hello. . . . Ah. You're hiding.

ROOFTOP: Not "hiding," juss not advertising.

FATHER LUX: Hiding.

ROOFTOP: You a funny cat, you know that?

FATHER LUX: If you're not hiding, take off the hat and glasses.

ROOFTOP: I am a grown man, Father—I believe I can attire myself as I please. . . .

FATHER LUX: Look you—Take off your hat and glasses.

ROOFTOP: Now Father, you a father, and a war veteran, cut off at the knees and all, and you ain't a bad guy, but—

FATHER LUX: Take off your hat and glasses or I'll turn around and leave right now.

Rooftop: Yeah, well, forgive me, Father, but that ain't much of a terrifying threat.

Father Lux: It's not? (*Beat.* **Rooftop** *takes off* **His** *shirt.*)

Rooftop: You an annoying mothahfuckah, and I don't feel no guilt saying it.

Father Lux: Look at me.

Rooftop: What? (**Father Lux** *extends* **His** *hands.*)

Father Lux: I want you to pray with me. Will you pray with me?

Rooftop: Pray? Goddamnit, Father—this is a bar—ain't no tabernacle!

Father Lux: You don't think God is here now?

Rooftop: I don't know.

Father Lux: God spends a lot more time here than he does next door.

Rooftop: Yeah, well, that explains a lot!

Father Lux: Take my hands now. Pray with me.

Rooftop: C'mon, man! I'm here with my peeps, took the damn red-eye, no sleep—

Father Lux: Say the Lord's Prayer with me. Would you do that?

Rooftop: For what?

Father Lux: Would you say the Lord's Prayer with me? Then I'll go. (*Beat.* **Rooftop** *takes* **Father Lux**'s *hands.*)

Rooftop: You a pest, Lux. Fuckin' pesty.

Father Lux: Okay . . . Ready?

ROOFTOP: How's that go again?

FATHER LUX: "Our father—"

ROOFTOP: Right, yeah, of course. . . .

FATHER LUX: Okay . . . Let's speak it silently, but together, and with care.

ROOFTOP: Right. Let's roll. (**THEY** *pray the Lord's Prayer silently . . .* **ROOFTOP** *and* **FATHER LUX** *regard each other.*)

FATHER LUX: I saw your ex-wife.

ROOFTOP: Inez?!

FATHER LUX: I mean, that's what this is all about, isn't it?

ROOFTOP: Where'd you see Inez at?

FATHER LUX: Is Inez what this is all about?

ROOFTOP: You didn't speak to her, did you?!

FATHER LUX: No.

ROOFTOP: Don't lie.

FATHER LUX: What made you decide to come to confession today?

ROOFTOP: Hold up! What was she doin' when you saw her?

FATHER LUX: Talking on her cell phone.

ROOFTOP: And how'd you know it was her?

FATHER LUX: Because it was her.

ROOFTOP: She had on that dark red dress?

FATHER LUX: Ah. You saw her too.

Rooftop: So?!

Father Lux: So, did you see her before or after you were suddenly overcome—after thirty years—with the desire for spiritual absolution?

Rooftop: Now dass . . . dass private!

Father Lux: . . . I will not leave without an answer.

Rooftop: Nah, man. Nah. (*Beat.*)

Father Lux: I'm not a good priest. I don't visit the sick because I'm afraid to go outside in my vestments. They won't let me say Mass anymore. I haven't left the rectory next door since I was transferred here nine months ago. And I don't want to. Black people scare me. I don't particularly like them. Or you, really. Most of the time, I don't believe in God at all, and when I do, I'm furious at Him . . . That's as honest as I can be. (*Beat.*)

Rooftop: I seen her before I came to see ya. She didn't see me, but I saw her. After she turned the corner, I opened up the car door and I vomited everything I had inside me onto the sidewalk— and I mean everything. My kidneys were flappin' against my ribs. My heart was pullin' against my chest. I tried to keep blowin' till my soul came up—just ta see if I still had one, but nothing came up, Father—nothin'. Just air . . .

Father Lux: I can fix that.

Rooftop: C'mon man, you a old, racist, tired, mothafuckin' pegleg mothahfuckah, you can't fix nothing.

Father Lux: If you really believed that, you wouldn't be sitting here. And you wouldn't have walked into my confessional this morning.

Rooftop: But Father . . .

Father Lux: Tell me everything you've ever done in your entire life that you feel killed your soul.

Rooftop: But that'll take days!

Father Lux: I don't have a problem with that. Do you?

MONOLOGUES FOR WOMEN

BEIRUT ROCKS
BY ISRAEL HOROVITZ

Nasa *and several other American college students take refuge in a downtown hotel when Israel attacks the city of Beirut in retaliation for the Hamas kidnapping of two Israeli soldiers in 2006. Tensions run high among the group of college students, and they suspect one of their friends,* Nasa, *simply because* She *comes from an Arab-American family. Despite some of the students' pleas for tolerance, other students—particularly a boy named Benjy—threaten to kill* Nasa *right then and there because they think* She *is a suicide bomber. When it turns out otherwise, they're naturally ashamed of what they threatened and how they humiliated* Her, *but* Nasa *delivers the following impassioned speech, enraged and in tears, to the others. This monologue can be performed by a man or a woman.*

Nasa: My family was killed by an Israeli missile that was fired from a tank into our house. I was two and a half. I had three older brothers. We lived in Gaza. My father owned a laundry. Many of his customers were Jews. One of his workers was a Jew. I'm told that my father hated politics. I'm told he was a peaceful man. He was killed, instantly, so were my brothers, my grandmother and grandfather. I was sleeping in a cot behind the house. They died. I didn't die. The Israelis thought there was a Hamas leader living in the house. They had the wrong address. They killed my family. Hamas paid for their burial. My mother's cousin came to collect me and take me back to America. All through high school, I thought the Palestinians were wrong. I thought Hamas was wrong. I thought I was American and the Israelis were the good guys. Last year, I began to think for myself, and I realized that I am not American. I am Palestinian. I am an Arab. I am studying my people's history, and learning my language. I want to know my family, my mother and father and brothers. I only have photographs and they look very nice.

(*To Benjy.*) You should have killed me, because I have a plan. I will be a martyr . . . I will honor my mother and father, I will honor my brothers, I will honor my grandparents. Sooner or later, it will happen.

(*In Arabic, chanted, loudly, head raised to Heaven.*) God is great. Hamas is great. Allah hu akbar. Hamas hu Akbar. Allah hu akbar. Hamas hu Akbar.

(*In English, to Benjy.*) You should kill me. If you don't, I will kill your family. Sooner or later, it will happen.

MARISOL
BY JOSÉ RIVERA

In this apocalyptic urban fantasy, Marisol has lost her job and joined the ranks of the homeless. Her guardian angel, however, has told Her of the revolt in heaven and asks Marisol to join her in overthrowing a tyrannous, old God and his shopworn rules that no longer apply to the modern world. As the play draws to a tense conclusion, Marisol is confused about taking sides, uncertain of Her own fate, and wandering in a dangerous world without Her moral compass. She delivers the following prayer to God, desperately hoping to find a spiritually valid answer to the pain, suffering, degradation, and filth in which Her world now seems to be drowning.

Marisol: Okay, I just wanna go home! Just wanna live with June—want my boring nine-to-five back—my two-weeks-out-of-the-year vacation—my intellectual detachment—my ability to read about the misery of the world and not lose a moment outta my busy day. To believe you really knew what you were doing, God—Please—if the sun would just come up! (*Beat. To herself.*) But what if the sun doesn't come up? And this is it? It's the deadline. I'm against the wall. I'm at the rim of the apocalypse . . . (Marisol *looks up. To the angel.*) Blessed guardian angel! Maybe you were right. God has stopped looking. We can't live life as if nothing's changed. To live in the sweet past. To look backwards for our instructions. We have to reach up, beyond the debris, past the future, spit in the eye of the sun, make a fist, and say no, and say no, and say . . . (*Beat. Doubts. To herself.*) No, what if she's wrong? (**SHE** *hurriedly gets on* **HER** *knees to pray. Vicious, to the crown.*) Dear God, All-Powerful, All-Beautiful, what do I do now? How do I get out of this? Do I have to make a deal? Arrange payment and bail myself out? What about it!? I'll do anything! I'll spy for you. I'll steal for you. I'll decipher strange angelic codes and mine harbors and develop germbombs and poison the angelic food supply. DEAR GOD, WHO DO I HAVE TO BETRAY TO GET OUT OF THIS FUCKING MESS?!

THE LARK

by JEAN ANOUILH

Translated by CHRISTOPHER FRY

The figure of Joan of Arc *has fascinated many playwrights for the past century and a half. One of the most famous portrayals of* Joan *comes from this play, which focuses intensely on the psychology of* Joan *and the loneliness that* She *must have felt during* Her *imprisonment. The actor must avoid presenting the piece quietly and contemplatively, reminiscing and delivering the lines as a vague, past recollection. Instead,* She *should approach the monologue more actively and enthusiastically, as a struggle to explain herself to the world—particularly in the section where* She *acts out* Her *encounter with Saint Michael—and as an exciting opportunity to share* Her *vivid spiritual experience with the audience.*

Joan: I like remembering the beginning: at home, in the fields, when I was still a little girl looking after the sheep, the first time I heard the Voices, that is what I like to remember. . . . It is after the evening Angelus. I am very small and my hair is still in pigtails, I am sitting in the field, thinking of nothing at all. God is good and keeps me safe and happy, close to my mother and my father and my brother, in the quiet countryside of Domrémy, while the English soldiers are looting and burning villages up and down the land. My big sheep-dog's lying with his head in my lap; and suddenly I feel his body ripple and tremble, and a hand seems to have touched my shoulder, though I know no one has touched me. I turned to look. A great light was filling the shadows behind me. The voice was gentle and grave. I had never heard it before, and all it said to me was: "Be a good and sensible child, and go often to church." But I *was* good, and I *did* go to church often, and I showed I was sensible by running away to safety. That was all that happened the first time. And I didn't say anything about it when I got home; but after supper I went back. The moon was rising; it shone on the white sheep; and that was all the light there was. And then came the second time; the bells were ringing for the noonday Angelus. The light came again, in bright sunlight, but brighter than the sun, and that time I saw him. A man in a white robe, with two white wings reaching from the sky to the ground. He didn't tell me his name that day, but later on I found out that he was the blessed St. Michael. (*In the deep voice of the Archangel.*) Joan, go to the help of the King of France, and give him back his kingdom. (**She** *replies in* **Her** *own voice.*) Oh sir, you haven't looked at me; I am only a young peasant girl, not a great captain who can lead an army.—You will go and search out Robert de Beaudricourt, the Governor of Vaucouleurs. He will give you a suit of clothes to dress you like a man, and he will take you to the Dauphin. St. Catherine and St. Margaret will protect you. (**She** *suddenly drops to the floor sobbing with fear.*) —Please, please pity me, holy sir! I'm a little girl; I'm happy here alone in the fields. I've never had to be responsible for anything, except my sheep. The Kingdom of France is far beyond anything I can do. If you will only look at me you will see I am small and ignorant. The realm of France is too heavy, sir. But the King of France has famous Captains, as strong as you could need, and they're used to doing these things. If they lose a battle they sleep as soundly as ever. They simply say the snow or the wind was against them;

and they just cross all the dead men off their roll. But I should always remember I had killed them. Please have pity on me! . . . No such thing. No pity. He had gone already, and there I was, with France on my shoulders. Not to mention the work on the farm, and my father, who wasn't easy.

THIS BEAUTIFUL CITY
BY STEVEN COSSON AND JIM LEWIS

In this docudrama, developed from interviews mainly with fundamentalist Christians in the community of Colorado Springs, characters speak directly to the audience as though explaining their lives and religious beliefs to the actors who originally interviewed them for the play. In the following monologue, set in a kids' playground, a young Christian woman calling herself "GOD'S GRACE" tries to tell us about HER struggle against intolerance and hatred of gay people. SHE even formed a study group at HER church to deal with the issue. SHE breaks down at the end, however, when HER father tests the limit of HER tolerance within HER own family, and snaps impatiently at HER children playing nearby.

GOD'S GRACE: Thanks for meeting me here. I just had to get the kids out of the house. What? (*Looking over at kids' playground.*) Oh, they're fine. OK, so I wanted to start the group at New Life, because I felt that Christians in general, have like this real nasty view towards homosexuality. I called my group "God's Grace and Homosexuality." Anyhow, I think it is important to have a forum where we could come together and discuss our love of these people but also not compromise our values. I just wanted to talk about it, you know? I mean there's got to be some middle ground between saying "You're a sinner and you're going to hell" and "Oh, everything you do is fine with me."

Yeah. I was kind of shocked that only two people showed up—I don't know. I felt like people were afraid to come. But who nowadays doesn't have someone in their life who's gay! My father is gay. He just celebrated his ten-year anniversary of his union. Yeah. My husband has learned to respect my dad. To be kind. But he doesn't want my dad staying at the house if he brings his lover with him. And my dad doesn't ask anymore. 'Cause you know for a long time my dad didn't respect our boundaries—you know. "Please! Don't make out with your boyfriend on the couch in front of my children! It's not OK! I don't want to have that talk with them just yet!" Yeah, he thought that because he was in love, and after all God is love, then we should just respect it. You know? (*Looking at kids.*) Oh guys! *Behave*, OK? Excuse me.

THIS BEAUTIFUL CITY
BY STEVEN COSSON AND JIM LEWIS

As in the previous monologue, this character speaks directly to the audience as though explaining HER life and religious beliefs to us. In this monologue, the young Christian housewife "GOD'S GRACE" speaks of HER religious conversion after emerging from HER dysfunctional family and a life of dissolution and self-indulgence.

GOD'S GRACE: We came from a Christian background. My father's father was a minister, so it was really a shock for all of us when my dad came out of the closet. So after my parents divorced I moved out here to live with my dad actually. I was just a kid and I wanted my dad, you know? I wanted him to keep loving me. But then my dad's boyfriend moved in. And I was put on the back burner; he didn't need me. So I just went wild and did whatever I wanted to. I actually met my husband when I'd just turned sixteen and within a few months I was living with him. . . . (*Kids in the distant background.*) Guys. Guys. Keep it down please. Mom is talking to someone. Anyhow, my husband and I lived in Manitou Springs then. (*A little quieter.*) There was constant drug use, for lack of a better way to put it. I can probably count the days of sobriety on two hands. My husband and I had a really short bout with crystal meth. And it must have been the grace of God, 'cause I've heard that it's really hard to get off of. And the day before, a Saturday night, my husband and I were actually at a strip club, a local strip club, and we were doing coke with a bunch of strippers—I dunno, it was a party night. We had a babysitter. And I guess I had just been very gently hearing God calling to me, because the next morning I got up, and I got the kids dressed, and I walked them to this church down the road, Revolution Church. Just like that, and it was funny. I mean, look where I'd been just a few hours before. And it was unlike anything I had ever been to. They had like strobe lights and a smoke machine and a disco ball! And the people there were my age and they had tattoos! And I was sitting there with my boys, and I felt that I just didn't realize that I had missed God! And I said, God, who am I to you? And He just revealed to me. "You are my daughter. You are the one who pleases me." And in a way it made me ashamed. But at the same time He just lifted that burden off of me. He freed me, and just revealed to me that it was OK. And it made His heart ache every time I made a poor choice, but He loved me nonetheless, and He wasn't willing to let me go. (*Wipes away tears*.) You know it's funny, that day if I had just walked into some boring church, I would still be sitting on the couch smoking pot. We really liked Revolution and are still really good friends with the leaders, but it went from being a church to being a twenty-four-hour house of prayer. Just prayer. All the time. By the time we had left it had gone from like a hundred and fifty members to twelve or something. We just needed more of a community. That's when we chose New Life. Yeah, Revolution House of Prayer.

ME AND JOAN (OF ARC)
BY KAREN SUNDE

Once again we see JOAN OF ARC, *but here* SHE's *portrayed delivering an inspired and stirring battle speech before* HER *army just prior to engaging the British forces. This is a "ladder" speech that rises steadily in emotional intensity, reaching a rousing climax in the final section of the monologue.*

JOAN: My friends. This sword has come to us from God. It is his sign. That we are right and we shall win.

But be not over-awed. And let your hearts beat softly in its light. He means to show, however small you are, however weak, when you will find his light, and stand within, your power will grow and blend with his.

So smile with me. We cannot fail. I stand before you, no more than a girl. But our country's pain moved me to cry to God, and God has sent this sword. And you will follow me. Each knowing I was nothing, as all, however mighty, are as nothing. But one as small as me, who with an open heart sees evil, and cries, "No. This must not be!" can make it so. For all God needs to battle evil, is one who loves enough to feel his power, and stand up unafraid.

So have no fear. What could we fear but death? And that God gives us, each one in his time, as he gives life. That time is not today. Today he needs our swords to win the mother back her child, his belly filled, his slumber soft and still. And we can do this thing for God. No matter how the giant enemy looms before us. For surely as we know we move with God, that giant will crumble at our approach, a rotten apple falling down, for nowhere in all the earth is there *any* power unless God gives it.

It is to us, today, he gives it. To know God's earthy sign to you, each place your hand upon your chest with me. (*Pause.*) Feel your heart pound against your honest palm? Now look to the man beside you. His is beating, too. And so is mine. And all belong to that same leap of joy—the quick'ning babe inside the mother's beat. And so we all can join! And when we do, we will together beat as God's own heart. And against this force . . . no siege can ever stand!

THE ARAB-ISRAELI COOKBOOK

BY ROBIN SOANS

The Arab-Israeli conflict, suicide bombers, and especially the motives of the women who sacrifice themselves for martyrdom, for revenge, or out of personal desperation—these are the subjects that the character FADI *contemplates in the following monologue. The piece is written to be spoken directly to the audience. And the structure of the monologue is challenging because it doesn't contain a central climax. Instead, it's built upon a series of smaller climaxes that the actress must identify and play as* FADI*'s story unfolds.*

FADI: No one is going to blow up the *Azkadinya*, or I don't think they are. You're not even searched when you go in. For a start it's in the Arab quarter . . . not that many Jewish people go there, so it's not an obvious target. And it has an international clientele, with a lot of diplomats, media people, TV correspondents, journalists. Even the terrorists don't want to antagonize the international community if they can help it. So I think the *Azkadinya*, reasonably safe . . . or that's what I thought until last Saturday . . . 'cos that's what I thought about *Maxim*'s, on the beach at Haifa. Every time I think about it, I get a rush of blood all round my body. If there's one place in Israel where there's been any hope, it's Haifa . . . a degree of Jews and Arabs living in harmony . . . finding a way of peaceable co-existence. And of all the places in Haifa, *Maxim's* was the most symbolic. It was co-owned by Jews and Arabs. I can't tell you how unusual that is . . . how encouraging . . . how progressive. I went there all the time . . . mostly to drink rather than to eat . . . it was nothing special as a restaurant; but what made it special was what it stood for . . . it's what me and my friends wanted to be part of . . . this attempt to buck the trend. I was on my way there . . . Saturday lunchtime . . . a friend planned to tell me . . . a suicide bomber had gone up to the security guard on the door, shot him dead, walked in, stood next to a baby's buggy . . . God, how out of love with humanity had this woman become . . . yes, it was a woman . . . a twenty-nine-year-old lawyer . . . she stood next to a baby's buggy, and detonated her bomb. My mother's dear friend, an old classmate, was killed. The force of the blast was enough to blow people's heads off. A baby's leg flew down to the edge of the sea, two hundred meters away. But however tragic it is to hear of body parts being blown to the winds . . . I don't know why God chose me for this, but he has given me the ability to see both sides of the situation, and, even among the so-called liberals here, there's no more than a handful of people who can do that. You see . . . this woman, this lawyer, in the previous three months her cousin, her brother, and I've been told her fiancé, had all been killed in Israeli army raids. For a woman from the Arabic culture, the ties to her male relatives are absolute . . . her loyalty, absolute . . . these ties are what give her strength, her energy, her status, absolutely her status in society . . . her reason to live if you like. To have one of these ties severed would be tragic; two, catastrophic; three . . . to have three destroyed . . . like . . . not in a natural disaster, but in violence . . . in conflict . . . she would be dehumanized—that's the word, dehumanized; there would be nothing left . . . except an overwhelming need to avenge blood and end her own life.

THE ARAB-ISRAELI COOKBOOK

BY ROBIN SOANS

Unlike in the previous monologue by Fadi from the same play, here the character RENA struggles to understand the tragic series of coincidences that led up to HER husband's death, and HER own responsibility for having unwittingly caused it. The structure of this monologue leads RENA closer and closer to the concrete details of HER husband's passing, until, by the end, SHE finds it difficult to continue speaking. But along the way, the actress must find short moments of desperate, black humor as RENA tries to relieve the painful grief SHE's experiencing.

RENA: Expansiveness is part of our nature. A place opens up, we go. When peace opened up with Egypt, we ran. "Hi, we're here, we're here, we're here." Did any Egyptians come here and say, "Hi, we're here, we're here, we're here"? No. The tourism was all one way, and not all Egyptians are poor. I'm very influenced by Agatha Christie. I said to Fred, "Do you know what I've always dreamed of doing? I'd love to sweep up to The Sphinx riding a camel, and wearing one of those big hats with a wide brim, looking like Vanessa Redgrave." And you know he did it . . . he hired the camel, bought the hat . . . we did it. (*The lights fade further. During HER next speech, RENA takes two candlesticks from a shelf, finds two candles to go in them from a drawer, finds a box of matches, lights the candles, and as* **She** *leaves, puts them on the table.*) Fred, my Fred. It's fourteen years, fourteen years ago tomorrow he died. I deal with it. I'm OK now. Life goes on. I cried and I cried and I cried, then I had a spectacular marriage. He was sexy . . . My God was he sexy. Every seven years the Julian and Gregorian calendars match up, which means that *Rosh Hashanah* falls on Friday, like this year . . . coincides with *Erev Shabbat* . . . makes it extra special. That Wednesday I was cooking. People kept calling, I don't know why . . . they just kept calling. "Our plans have fallen through, can we come to you?" "Can we come, can we come?" I said to Fred, "We haven't got enough food . . . I need some more vegetables, I need some more peas, I need some more honey." He said, "I'll take care of it, you just carry on cooking." I said, "If you're going to the supermarket, the tickets never arrived from the Synagogue," and he said, "It's only across the street, I'll pick them up at the same time." He was crossing the street from the supermarket to the Synagogue. There was a guy driving a white van so fast he lost control . . . killed him . . . he died in my arms in the hospital. He never regained consciousness. The police called, "Your husband's had a little accident, he's in the emergency ward, get in a cab and come over." Do you know the strangest thing? It never occurred to me 'til later. Why did they say, "Get in a cab"? I called my girlfriend, and told her Fred had had an accident, and the police had told me to get in a cab and go to the hospital. It didn't occur to her either. If it was a little accident, why didn't I just get in my own car? Of course, if I had, I would never have been able to drive back. I was convinced he'd broken his leg; I took a book; I thought, I'm going to be there for hours while they put his leg in plaster. When I got there, this doctor I've known a long time told me to come and say goodbye. I had Fred in my arms . . . the doctor put his hand on my shoulder,

"Let him go, Rena, let him go." I said, "It's OK, I love you. You can go in peace." I let him go and he died. I always believe he was waiting for me, for at that exact instant he died. Fred died two days before *Rosh Hashanah*.

GIDION'S KNOT

BY JOHNNA ADAMS

An eleven-year-old child has killed himself as a result of the rejection he experienced in school by his teacher and his classmates. Following his death, his teacher, MRS. CLARK, reads his last essay to the boy's grieving mother, who has come to his classroom for a parent-teacher conference. It was the boy's essay that upset the other students and his teacher. MRS. CLARK finds his writing extremely painful at many points, yet struggles to temper HER personal responses out of respect for the boy's mother, who is listening.

MRS. CLARK: "It began during a war, as things do. We all formed tribes and began killing the teachers. I cut Mr. Shawn apart myself with a hunting knife my grandfather gave me the last time he took me hunting for ravens. We needed his entrails for our weavers and our poets. I think Mr. Shawn was grateful. A group of sixth graders had caught him in the cafeteria earlier, by the vending machines, and cut out his eyes, flayed him and raped him with the clubs they had fashioned by cutting the dicks off of their fathers and stretching the skin over thick poles. He was spitting up blood because of something they'd broken in him and I think he loved me for cutting him open. I took a broomstick out of the janitor's closet and nailed one end of his intestines to it and then rolled the rest of his intestines out of his stomach, twisting them around the broomstick—

they stretched more than twenty-five feet when I was done. Mr. Shawn had told me that intestines were that long in science class a month ago, but I didn't believe him until we started collecting them for the weavers and the poets. He was lucky. Most kids wouldn't have killed him first. I put the thick roll of Mr. Shawn's intestines over my shoulder and started walking to the gym, which is the room where we kept the weavers. Outside of Ms. Harris's room, a tribe of fifth graders were raping Ms. Clark, Ms. Tologos, and Ms. Harris. The boys were raping them, the girls were slowly slicing away their nipples with vegetable peelers they'd won in the great cafeteria war against the lunch ladies. These kids didn't want anything more than this. They didn't care about the weavers or poets. So they left the teachers raped and scarred and blind, but didn't take their entrails. So I killed Ms. Tologos and Ms. Harris and rolled their entrails onto the broomstick with Mr. Shawn's. It was harder with Ms. Clark. They'd left her one eye and she was watching me. She was naked and they'd taken her nipples, her tongue, and she was so ripped apart down there, it looked like dogs had been at her and not just kids. But, I really needed her entrails. More than she did at this point. So I put my knife in her remaining eye and twisted it into her brain. And I rolled her entrails up with the rest. Around the corner in the hall outside the nurse's office, the nurse, Carole from the office, and the fat principal were hanging from the walls by nails punched through their wrists and ankles and knees and shoulders. Their bodies were just gaping empty bags. No entrails to salvage. And then I saw Jake Powell. Jake's tribe and their first grade slaves. That was the truly sick thing. Jake was raping the same first grade kid he had been raping even before the war began. You all already knew about that. This dumb little kid with glasses. Jake used to have to sneak around about it, but with the teachers dead or dying, he could do what he pleased. I watched him torture his first grade slaves for a while—he maimed and raped and bled and squeezed and screamed and sucked and chewed and twisted. Even before the war Jake was wrong. When the weavers give me my cloak, maybe I can do something about him. The broomstick was heavy and I had enough guts, so I made my way to the gym, where the weavers worked. Since the weavers started working, the gym stopped smelling like a gym and started smelling like a butcher's shop and a toilet. All those entrails being braided and woven. You wondered how the weavers could stand it, but when they changed into weavers, maybe they lost their sense of smell. We had been in home period, in Ms. Clark's room when the first weaver was chosen. We don't know by who, some think there are aliens on earth like the body snatchers and some think God did it. But whoever did it, in the middle of class this girl suddenly screamed and her eyes turned into balls of blue glass and her arms stretched out like poles and her hands grew new fingers and grew big. This was happening in other classes, but we didn't know that. And she started asking for entrails. Not to eat but to make things with. So we put her and the others in the gym and they started making looms out of the janitor's supplies. And we started killing for them. We had to give the weavers what they needed. Some of us sort of hung back to see what the weavers were making from the teachers' entrails before we started killing and gutting. But when the first cloak was made and the first poet climbed the hill, I knew I had to kill however many teachers I needed to so that I could have one. I gave a weaver my last pile of entrails and she tied them onto the ends of the other entrails I had brought her and started weaving. The cloth the weavers make from the teachers' entrails is like nothing you've ever seen. It's like a river and a taste of salt. It's like an ocean with fish moving through the black water.

When the weaver finished my gut-cloak she put it around my shoulders and I felt the pull. And I walked out of the building to the soccer field where the tribes who kept the first through third grade kids as slaves had made them build a mountain. And I climbed the mountain and joined the poets there. We watch the war and we write about the great deeds done or the horrors done. And that is how God remembers you—the way we write you. And no other way. He was passing it around. To the other students. It's my responsibility to— . . . . I'm sure you understand. I'm sure you understand now.

MONOLOGUES FOR MEN

WAKE ME WHEN IT'S OVER
BY SYBIL ST. CLAIRE

This piece contains a lot of built-in theatricality for the actor to physicalize: the ritual of kneeling at a wake and attempting to recite prayers, the queasy stomach, the shocking realization and reversal of tone and subject, and the shaft of illumination. Best of all, it's written to be spoken naturally, directly to the audience. One shouldn't be put off by the mournful occasion at the beginning because, like a TV commercial, the monologue does an abrupt about-face halfway through, making the earlier seriousness seem almost comical. At the beginning of the piece, the playwright suggests that the GIRL/BOY kneel facing the audience, cross himself or herself, and attempt to pray. SHE/HE looks as though SHE/HE has indigestion. This monologue can be performed by either a male or a female actor.

GIRL/BOY: (*An offering to the audience.*) Green bean casserole? It's Day Three. My grandfather, the diabetic, just downed a fifth of jack with one hand and gave himself a shot of insulin with the other. Aunt Be wanted to show me how her colostomy bag worked, and my cousin, who failed homeschooling, just barfed all over the baby Jesus. Then there's my grandmother. (*Crossing self,* SHE/HE *kneels in front of a casket, purposely avoiding looking inside*.) She's dead. (*Crosses self again*.) Day Three. Irish wake.

I don't wanna look. She's my grandmother, the woman who acted as if it was perfectly normal that I wanted to sleep with a live turtle until I was twelve. The woman who taught me bird calls, and how to butterfly tie my shoes, and to never, ever eat spaghetti on a first date. She was always teaching me stuff. Day Three and I haven't . . . (**She/He** *accidentally looks down into the casket—silence.* **She/He** *leans farther forward—confusion— then:*) That is not my grandmother. That doesn't even look like my grandmother. They always look like they're sleeping on TV! She's not sleeping. She's not there. I mean it's her body but . . . (*A revelation.*) she's not in it.

(*Crosses self again, tries to pray. No good.*) This Catholic stuff is hard work. We have to train to be forgiven. "Body and blood of Christ." (**She/He** *mimes a priest giving the host.*) There's an actual class for that. And it tastes like crap and it sticks to the roof of your mouth and you can't get it off cause you're not allowed to tongue Jesus. It's a complex and confusing religion that never once gave me comfort, or direction, or inspiration. And I never really believed in any of it anyway. But this. . . . (**She/He** *indicates the grandmother's body.*) This I can believe in. Not in a Vatican, genuflect, stigmata kinda way but in a, "There really is something beyond this" kinda way. I mean, obviously, the body must just be some kind of crash pad for the soul. A place to call home while we're in the hood . . . and one day the lease runs out and the soul moves on. Damn! (**She/He** *looks heavenward.*) Sorry, Grandma. (*With a smile.*) You're just always teaching me stuff.

BENGAL TIGER AT THE BAGHDAD ZOO
BY RAJIV JOSEPH

TIGER is played by a male actor making no attempt whatsoever to physicalize the voice or movements of an animal. In this scene he's TIGER's ghost, having been shot earlier in the play by a US soldier and now wandering the streets of Baghdad, encountering the souls of other animals and humans killed in the conflict. The playwright uses TIGER to pose theosophical questions about a loving God, the meaning of life, and the hereafter. Here, TIGER tells the audience about HIS strange meeting with the spirit of a little girl recently killed. The topiary garden to which TIGER refers was an actual garden cultivated by Saddam Hussein's son Uday, but the plants are now blasted and burned by the war.

TIGER: This place is lousy with ghosts.

And the new ones are irritating. They're walking around, wide-eyed. . . . *What happened to me? Where am I?*

You're dead and you're in Baghdad. Shut up.

Anyhow, the other day, I'm walking down the street. The street is literally *on fire*.

And I see this little girl. Her life is like a soap bubble, and then pop!

She's here, in the middle of the street, looking up at me. And she says to me: What are you? And I tell her, I'm a tiger.

She asks me am I going to eat her.

And I say, no, I gave up eating little children.

She says why?

And I say, I don't know, it's this philosophy I'm working out about sin and redemption because God is apparently nuts.

And the girl just kind of looks at me.

And I'm like, think about it, if God's watching, why'd he snuff you out? Why are you standing here, alone, in a burning street, with a dead tiger?

Why is half your face gone?

And she says yeah, but why'd you give up eating children?

And I tell her the bit about the two kids in the forest, and how I keep thinking about them and how I have all this guilt.

She doesn't understand that. The guilt thing. She doesn't have any guilt. And I'm like, of course you don't. What did you ever do? Nothing.

She tells me she's afraid.

I tell her I am too.

Which you'd think would be comforting, given the circumstances, but somehow, being blown to bits and then coming face-to-face with the likes of *me*. . . .

Well, the girl starts to cry, you know?

Her one eye cries.

And I say, don't cry. But she cries harder. And so I say to her, hey do you want to see something? And she stops crying for a second. And she's like, what?

And I say it's a . . . I tell her it's a garden.

And she looks at me as if to say, big fucking deal, like I haven't seen a garden before?

And I say, no it's a special garden. (*Lights up on the topiary animals.*) And I don't know why I say this, but I say, it's God's garden.

I tell her it's God's garden.

He likes gardens, see. He tests us in them, he tempts us in them, he builds them up and tears them apart. It's like his fucking hobby.

And she's skeptical, I can see that, but I bring her here and she sees these plants, these animals, and she's never seen anything like them. And I nailed it because she's not crying any more. She's walking around the garden, pointing. *A lion! A camel! An elephant!*

Fucking kids, you know?

And I mean, this whole time I'm talking out of my ass, this business about God's garden, etcetera. Maybe she knows I'm bullshitting too. The girl is no dummy, even if she does only have half a brain.

But for a second we both look up at these ruined shrubs and think, okay Man, you work in Mysterious Ways. We get it.

And I feel this swell of hope.

And then she turns to me and she's like, *When will he get here?*

What?

She says, *When will God get here? If this is His garden, then He has to come to it, He has to tend it.*

Look! She says. *Green is all burned.*

This animal has lost his head.

Well?!

What am I supposed to tell her?

I'm asking You to tell me.

Because if You don't . . . I'm going to have to watch her cry again. I'm gonna have to sit here and watch that little single eye of hers well up with tears. . . .

Until eventually she'll stop. She'll stop crying.

And her brain will fill up, as mine did, and she'll understand the universe.

And her spirit or body or whatever You've left us with, it will go on to other things.

And this moment, *this fucking moment* when she appraises a ruined piece of beauty with her one good eye, *this moment* will become extinct.

Just like You.

Is that what You *want? Say something! This animal has lost her head!* Speak through me, or through her, or through someone, but speak, God, speak!

THE CONTROVERSY OF VALLADOLID

BY JEAN-CLAUDE CARRIÈRE

During the sixteenth century, BROTHER BARTOLOME DE LAS CASAS *was galvanized by the hideous persecution and torture of the native tribes that he witnessed in the New World, as the first Bishop of Chiapas (Mexico). When the Pope finally called an official investigation into the practices of the Spanish conquistadores, it was* LAS CASAS *who argued forcefully in Valladolid, Spain, against the rapacious practices of the Spanish troops in the name of Christ. In the following scene,* HE *addresses the court, which consists largely of the Papal Legate.*

LAS CASAS: Eminence, our Lord Jesus Christ said: "I am the truth and the life." I will try to speak the truth about those who continue to this day to lay waste to human life. (*Short pause.*) The truth is: at this very moment we are killing them. Ever since the discovery and conquest of the Indies, the Spanish have not stopped enslaving, torturing, massacring the Indians. (HE *pats a pile of papers.*) Where to begin? The extent of this horror—it could fill volumes. From the moment they arrived, the Spanish have been consumed by an unrestrained thirst for gold. For fifty years, since finding this deadly metal dangling from these natives' ears. Since then, it has been: gold. Gold! Give me gold! I have heard natives ask, what do they do with all that gold? Eat it? Rather it's the gold that has eaten them, as well as the unfortunate Indians who from the beginning have been treated like mindless beasts. (**He** *picks up a file, starts to open it, then closes it, preferring to speak without notes.*) From the beginning, they were branded—on Cortez's orders. Today, branded with their owner's name. Sold from owner to owner, branded again and again, brand upon brand, until their faces— like old pieces of writing paper. (**He** *takes out some drawings from the files and shows them.*) From the beginning, they died by the thousands in the mines. Worse than hell, these mines, dark, wet, and with an unGodly stench. Vultures circling above, so many they hide the sun. (**Las Casas** *has become quite animated.*) Millions have been massacred. Yes, millions! Like beasts in a slaughterhouse. Any way. Every way. Mostly with a blade, gunpowder costs too much. I've seen them impaled on spits in groups of thirteen, set over fires and cooked. Or hands hacked off, then released in the woods and told to "spread the word." I'm telling you the truth. The Lord has been "honored" by the horrors of these men. What have they not done? Children held by their feet and swung. Their skulls cracked against a wall or rock. Or cooked alive, or drowned, or thrown to starving dogs who bite into them like hogs. Bets made on who could disembowel a woman in a single stroke. These people are not at war! They came to us—smiling, their faces open, interested in us, laden with fruits, presents. And we brought to them their death. In the name of God, no less. Death. Eminence, Christians have lost their fear of God. They have forgotten who they are. Yes, millions of them! Maybe more. In the cities of Cholula and Tapeaca, entire populations had their throats cut! To the cry of "Saint James!" They couldn't understand who we were or what we wanted. We made no sense to them. As Columbus himself said, the first time he saw them: "I cannot believe there are better men on earth." They are beautiful, Eminence, in every way. They are peaceful, as gentle as sheep. They want nothing from you. Generous, open. With total openness. They cannot lie. So they are easily tricked. I cannot say it better: they were the picture of Paradise before the fall.

THE CONTROVERSY OF VALLADOLID

BY JEAN-CLAUDE CARRIÈRE

During the sixteenth century, GINES DE SEPULVEDA *was appointed by the Spanish crown to defend the hideous persecution and torture of the native tribes in the New World by Spain's military forces. As an educated nobleman,* HE *believed that the native tribes were subhuman and needed to be "converted" to Christianity by force and by enslavement. In a famous ecclesiastical debate in Valladolid, Spain,* HE *defended the rapacious policies of slavery imposed by the conquistadores. In the following scene,* SEPULVEDA *addresses the court, consisting largely of the Papal Legate, and Bishop Bartolome de Las Casas, who is arguing on the side of the native inhabitants of the Americas and against their enslavement.*

GINES DE SEPULVEDA: Spain will be praised for having rid the earth of such a bloodthirsty and cursed species. For having brought a few to the side of the true God. For having tried to teach them what we know. I believe it. I strongly believe it. The Indies won't be abandoned. That is fantasy. We'll stay there. History moves forward, not backward. The question here is that which philosophy has always addressed: What should we do, what can we do? (*To Las Casas.*) As you said yourself, we should convert them into Christians. Without this, no good can come to them in this life, or the next. How then to convert them? How long will it take? At what price? This is the second part of the question, and it is on this point, Brother Bartolome, that we differ. (*Another pause, to make* **His** *point, then to Las Casas.*)

You say, both Christians and slaves is impossible. That the two are mutually exclusive. I say: Why is that? At least in the short term, while waiting for the complete conversion. And what shall we do with those who don't want to be Christians? I'll let Saint Luke answer you, in words first spoken by Christ: *Compelle eos intrare.* Force them to enter. How then to force them to enter? By keeping them slaves for a while and explaining: those who sincerely wish to be Christian shall *ipso facto* no longer be slaves. Here then is our primary moral duty. I say that a just war is one fought for justice. The conquest proved—if proof were needed—the validity of our Christian faith. It is well known that the Muslims, having spread their evil over a vast empire for centuries, are now weakened. Every indication is that their end is near. Yes, I too am one of those who think the reign of the true faith is near. I believe it will soon be established here on earth. And that it will last a thousand years. Would you want to exclude them from it? (*Pause.*) Which is the greater good? (**He** *pauses. Silence.*) You speak through Saint Paul, I answer through Saint Augustine. The greatest good is the salvation of the soul. The loss of one single unbaptized soul, said Saint Augustine, is worse than the mortal death of countless victims, themselves innocent. That is why we work so hard to convert them. Otherwise their souls are lost. And nothing in this world, or the next, is more precious than the soul. Every text of the Church, Father, affirms this: anyone, be he Muslim, Jew, Buddhist, savage, who is not baptized, anyone, without exception, will be thrown into the eternal fires and burned without ever being destroyed. (*A pause.*) This is why true Christians step forward, taking such pains to bring the true word to the new world. To save them! To save their soul! To give them the chance at eternal life! Don't misunderstand me. (*Pause.*) I'm not saying they have souls like ours, of the same quality, or even near it, and there is no reason to treat them like us. (*Another pause.*) But in case I am mistaken, which is possible, in case Aristotle is mistaken, and their souls are like ours, then I still say a soul is creation's most precious pearl, that it must be saved at all cost. (**HE** *moves forward for* **HIS** *final words, becoming strong, persuasive, though also menacing.*) Which is better: a long wasted life on earth, lived in error and sin, followed by an eternity of suffering? Or a much shorter life here, probably much harder, and an early death, but followed by the eternal light of the true conquering God?! (*Pause.*) Is there anyone here who doesn't know the answer?

PILGRIMS MUSA AND SHERI IN THE NEW WORLD
BY YUSSEF EL GUINDI

ABDALLAH *has been living in New York and earning a lot of money helping fellow Muslim immigrants adjust to the "new world." Recently,* HE *has drowned in a ferry accident while on a pilgrimage to Mecca to give thanks to Allah for* HIS *success in America. But here, at the end of the play,* HIS *soul returns once more to* HIS *dingy Manhattan apartment, where* HE *reflects one last time on the spiritual discoveries* HE *made as an immigrant to the United States.*

ABDALLAH: One more look. Before my body washes ashore and they bury me. Before they find my suitcase floating and identify me. Look where my memory—my spirit, takes me. To *this* place. To the struggles I had here. I went—I traveled to give thanks. To walk with strangers gathered for something. To walk in what I knew would be a crush of too many people gathered to give thanks. A coming together. Of people from everywhere; with different tongues and looks and ways of seeing things. And for all of us to remember a time before we were—before we were strangers to each other. To connect, and pull our voices together in song and reflect upon the paths our hearts have stumbled along. And here: the country I came to. The strangers I met here. The everyday pilgrimage you make when you open your mouth to a stranger and hope to God you are understood. The everyday Kaaba you walk around, the everyday Mecca you head towards. The people you meet who don't know you. The way you have to open up and travel to the place someone is coming from. Before my body washes ashore, I remember that; not the immigrant I was, but the pilgrim I became by coming here. The riches I was gathering even before the money started coming in. Learning of the dreams we shared, the same search I had as all these other people. *These* riches.

GOLDEN CHILD
BY DAVID HENRY HWANG

TIENG-BIN *is a wealthy Chinese man with three wives, but* HE *has been away from China, living in the Philippines for three years on business, and has just returned. This scene with* HIS *parents precedes a homecoming dinner with* HIS *favorite wife, Eling, who will mock* HIS *recent adoption of modernized "Christian" values while* HE *has been living in Manila. Here,* HE *struggles to explain to* HIS *very conservative and traditional Buddhist parents some of the recent spiritual changes that have occurred in* HIS *life as a result of* HIS *contact with Christianity.*

TIENG-BIN: Papa, Mama, Ankong, Ama—I know I haven't been the most diligent son lately. (**HE** *kowtows, burns paper money.*) But how can I explain—what it is like for me to work in the modern world—and then return here, to my home village, where everything remains as you and your fathers decided it should be? Can you possibly understand—you who lived your entire lives within the boundaries of this country hamlet, so far removed from any threat to your old way? (*Pause.*) Then what do I do with my doubts? Questions concerning the very traditions you taught me? When I was young, Papa, you would order me to obey, and your strong hand put an end to all discussion. How much simpler life was in those days. (**HE** *pulls out a small crucifix, displays it to the altar.*) I bought a souvenir for you in a

Christian temple in the Philippines. A naked man nailed to some boards. They told me for good luck, you can kiss its feet. They're very strange, the Westerners, and yet—hopeful, too. All the time talking about new inventions, new ideas. Nothing seems to excite them more than the future. Well, I must prepare for the banquet. Don't worry, I am still a good son. I go through all the motions, and curse myself for every deviation. In the house of his birth, a man is always a child.

IN THE SHAPE OF
A WOMAN
BY TAMMY RYAN

This monologue focuses on the voice of our conscience: how difficult it is to listen to it and to follow its advice, how easily we lose sight of it, and how we need to respect it as a holy power within each of us. The time is medieval France, the trial and execution of Joan of Arc. JEAN BREHAL is a high churchman, the Inquisitor of France, who conducted the inquiry into Joan of Arc's first trial following her death. In the original play, the role was played by a female actress, "doubling" in this role of BREHAL, although the monologue can be effectively spoken by either a man or a woman.

JEAN BREHAL: I had a voice once. I wasn't sure at first it was a voice. It came to me as a thought. About how I wanted to live my life. How I should change my surroundings and live a different life, a life that honored God. Sometimes the voice was not a voice, sometimes it was a feeling. A nagging urge in a certain direction that gave me no peace until I followed it. Sometimes it's been quiet, barely a whisper, easy to ignore, other times it's been loud, all consuming, forcing me to act. Sometimes I think I've seen it, like, "a great multitude of very small things." And each small thing is a choice you can make, shining there in front of you, waiting for you to choose it, follow it, sacrifice your brief, unimportant, shallow but sacred life only to it. If it means suffering, if it means dying. That kind of voice. (*Looks at Joan to see if* **He***'s right.*) It's never formed words for me, although it was sometimes a sound, in the echo of things, in the buzzing of things. Sometimes it's a sound you hear, other times it's a sound you make, you sing it or dance it or write it or fight it or pray it or give birth to it. Sometimes you are the sound. You are the voice. (*Whispers furiously.*) How do we lose it? How do we get it back? How do we make our peace with it, keep it in our hearts and make it holy?

THIS BEAUTIFUL CITY
BY STEVEN COSSON AND JIM LEWIS

In this docudrama, developed from interviews mainly with fundamentalist Christians in the community of Colorado Springs, characters speak directly to the audience as though explaining their lives and religious beliefs to the actors who originally interviewed them for the play. In the following section, a middle-aged air force VETERAN *expresses* HIS *anger toward what* HE *regards as a flagrant violation of the US Constitution by the US Armed Forces, and by the evangelical chaplains* HE *encountered there. In the middle of* HIS *story,* HE *takes an imaginary question from the audience.*

VETERAN: Look, I don't know what you're going for with your show if you're shooting for G or PG 'cause with me you're going to get the R version and maybe some X. OK? OK. So, for the record, I was Air Force. . . . So, um, I think I know a little of what I'm talking about. And let me tell you, the line between the church and the state's armed forces has been completely dissolved. Go back to your hometown paper and read the July 12, 2005, front page of the *New York Times*. General Richardson, the number two ranking chaplain in the Air Force, makes an astonishing fucking statement. Front page *New York Times*. It's the Air Force's official policy to evangelize anyone who comes into the service who is "unchurched." You know, my wife and I have three kids in the US Air Force. And we're Jewish. Now, do our kids fall into this category being unchurched? And if so, Air Force, are you going to exercise your fucking right to evangelize them? . . . *Look, I do not care what they believe.* Even though these are people that believe that Jack Benny, Dr. Seuss, Gandhi, and Anne Frank are burning in an eternal fiery lake of hell. (*Question.*) Jack Benny? He was Jewish. And last I heard Anne Frank was. If you want to believe that little girl is roasting in hell, I'll support you with the last fiber of my being under our social contract to believe that. But if you try to engage in the power of the state, and in the armed forces, and have my government tell me who are the children of the greater God and who are the children of the lesser God, I will fucking kill you or I will go down trying.

IN A KINGDOM BY THE SEA
BY KAREN SUNDE

In this docudrama, HOGAN is a marine colonel who was abducted and killed in South Lebanon while trying to rescue some fellow Americans. In this life-after-death monologue, HE struggles to reflect on the circumstances that brought HIM here, to death, and begins to wonder how HE might change HIS values in HIS next incarnation, after passing through this fuzzy gray world of souls like HIS who have recently died.

HOGAN: You know that moment, Sami, very early, fuzzy gray, when you open your eyes and don't know who you are? I sometimes teeter there, wanting to start new, but if I shut my eyes again, it always happens: I find Todd.

And I promise her, next time we'll know why, there'll be a reason. Not because we don't know the first thing about who the hell people in what the hell country we've set our fat fanny down in!

But mostly I lie there in the fuzzy gray, you know how it is? Just part of that gray that's barely light at all, with nothing . . . attached to you, no memory of who is it you're supposed to be. That moment is so soft.

You think—did I have problems? Something I had to do? Someone I cared for? Then all the attachments return to make you a skin. You're the hero! You can get up. You forget it ever happened. It's just a moment . . . between dreaming you're someone else and knowing you aren't.

But I always wonder. . . . Maybe that fuzzy gray moment was the real one? If I can just get back to it, I'll figure things out differently. Hell, I'm no ace in this heroes business. I thought, "work a quick deal, release a few Americans." Damned if I know what I was trying to. . . . Seems like I'm leading a parade that turned the corner five blocks back! But I'm the hero. Aren't I?

So I think I *could* start new, floating there in the barely gray morning. I just need to . . . pull my skin on a little . . . differently.

A TUESDAY IN APRIL
BY MAX BUSH

Is religious faith a lunatic's fantasy, a normal human attribute, a challenging attitude that is everywhere contested these days, or perhaps just another manifestation of pop culture swirling about us like the broken and abandoned icons floating in a sea of cultural-historical "wreckage" from societies past and present? Earlier selections in this anthology, such as Agnes of God, Marisol, In the Shape of a Woman, *and others, explored the boundaries of religion and human psychology. In this monologue, we see a psychologist,* CRAIG, *struggling to make sense of* HIS *patients' ravings and in doing so, asking himself important questions about the nature of human belief.*

CRAIG: (CRAIG *takes a drink, turns to the recorder, stares at it.* HE *moves to* HIS *desk, turns on the recorder.*) Self indulgent. (HE *switches it off.*) Yep. Even now. (*Short silence.*) Yep. (HE *switches it on again.*) Well, a short story first. I remember—far too much—but I remember in one of my earlier hospitalizations a man—and this is to explain an important point about us—a man about twenty-four—greasy hair, white skin, blue hospital gown—sitting still in the day room as we are prone to do—especially in the spring. I just couldn't take this guy's pain. And obviously the staff wasn't helping him; maybe he'd respond to a fellow patient. So I went over to sit with him, to help him. That's how much I believed in the laying-on of hands in those days. I sat with him, hoping he would speak first, which, of course, he didn't. Finally I asked him what was wrong.

"Why are you so sad?"

And he said: "I'm dead." (**CRAIG** *smiles*.)

"Do you mean you're dead?" I asked.

"Yes, I'm dead."

So I thought of a way to help him. I asked: "Do dead people bleed?"

"No, that's ridiculous," he said.

So I took him to my room where I had hidden a small knife. I pricked his finger and said: "Look at that."

He looked up and said: "I'll be damned, dead people do bleed."

An old joke. But you understand—we do bleed but it doesn't really help. (*Pause.*) You know I can see the world out there. God, it's a serious place: red lights, laundry, insurance, library fines, driving to the dentist's office, or to meet a father. Supper. Brief cases. (*Pause.*) And then there is the story of the woman who was too much in love with her son. This isn't what you're thinking. She believed creatures that had escaped from hell buried magnets around her house that had the power to attract the souls of children. The creatures would then trade the souls they'd caught to the Devil for more time on earth. When this mother couldn't explain the four-year-old boy's constant crying and fatigue, she thought he was fighting being drawn into the magnets. And so, in an act of love—as she knew there was no escaping the pull of the magnets—she poisoned her son, then herself. She lived. He didn't. Now she prays every other night for forgiveness and every other night that he escaped the magnets and ascended to heaven. The point is, of course, that it was an act of love, the freeing of a spirit. Those of us who aren't immune to the magnets need to be cut from this earth . . . in an act of love . . . Leana. (*Pause.*) Then there is the story of the other guy who thought he was Jesus. Christ, I couldn't believe someone would really admit he was Jesus. One day, in early April—on a day very much like today—I went to him and asked, "J. Christ?"

"Yes," he smiled, delighted that I recognized him.

"Prepare ye the way," I warned, "anoint thyself with oil for verily I say unto you tomorrow is Good Friday."

"Good Friday!"

Terrified he ran to his room and prayed all day, all night. The next morning he emerged in glory, naked, full of purpose, knowing who we are and what we need to do, ready to die for the world's sins. (*Silence.*) He was disappointed the next day . . . relieved, too . . . All right, maybe he wasn't Jesus. Hope again, see? But neither did he rise on the third day full of God's light, reborn unto the spirit. Maybe he's an older, sadder God. The Sacrificial Fool, to be tied to an oak and rent . . . slowly . . . over the time of his life. (*Silence.*) A couple of weeks later I noticed Jesus dancing and singing in the day room. His beard was shaggy, his hair was unkempt—all this was strangely different for him. Thinking the meds had finally straightened him out, I asked: "Are you feeling better?" "You taught me something important." He smiled. "It's amazing how we can delude ourselves. I thought I was Jesus. Can you believe it? Me, Jesus! I'm dancing, see? I say 'fuck' all the time, and I'm in love with three nurses. I'm obviously the Anti-Christ!" . . . Thinking quickly, I took his arm and led him down the hall to the new patient on the ward, a fiftysomething still dressed in his Sunday clothes and forever carrying his Bible. I said to the new patient: "Who are you?"

"I am the anti-Christ."

"You too?"

I left them alone to work it out . . . that was pretty crazy . . . But not as crazy as, let's say, getting a running start and slamming yourself into a cement wall; I've seen that. Or . . . eating a newspaper. That's pretty crazy. Or carrying on a conversation with a floor lamp . . . When I was bored in the hospital I used to form catatonics into famous paintings. "Afternoon in the Park." "The Creation of Man." "American Gothic." "The Statue of Liberty." That was kind of crazy . . . The crazy doctor! One day we had a naturalist tell us schizophrenia and maybe even depression could be cured with vitamin therapy. And, along with a pocketful of vitamins he prescribed, every day, twenty tablets of Unjointed, Dehydrated Wheat Grass . . . with a digestive aid of Ox Bile. Even the schizophrenics knew how crazy that was. Nothing came of it except one of the psychotics pierced his nose with a large ring. (*Short silence.*) Schizophrenics, as you know, have problems with their bowels. Because of the drugs. Once we hoarded the laxatives for a week and one morning we put them in the staff coffee pot. That got pretty crazy . . . Psych-types are such tight-assed bastards they didn't say anything to each other. It was hours of amusing insanity. "Mr. Van Sloten, I'd like to take your blood pressure now. But . . . I'm afraid I don't have time. I have an unexpected meeting I must attend. Immediately." And then in group lobotomy—all the paranoids and even the major depressives showed up—even the woman who thought she was a dog trotted in. Not a patient left the room. But the staff leading the group—like an anxious tag team at a wrestling match. God, we laughed all morning. (*Silence. Suddenly intensely.*) It's just that I can't call the world to me, and even if I did, who would come?—all right, even if you came what would you do? Give me to the doctors—tell me your story—tell me your story—tell me your story—we all have stories! Mine's not even that horrible! Then drugs! Then art! Then music! Then group after group after group after group! And then, when I'm not looking, suddenly I can see. I can see NOW. I can see where I am and I am not the world's keeper. And that makes it worse because I know it will end, which it does, and I know NOW is out there, which it is, and I can do nothing to get it back. (*Turning to door.*) No? Then we all agree. And I have to do this while I still l can. But first, one last story. "A Tuesday in April," I call it.

SPEAKING WELL OF THE DEAD

BY ISRAEL HOROVITZ

It doesn't take much to awaken pangs of horror and outrage at the atrocity committed on September 11, 2001, in New York City by Al-Qaeda terrorists. This short monologue omits explicit mention of the epic details of the disaster and focuses instead on a small BOY *who lost* HIS *father that day. The* BOY *deals with* HIS *loss and* HIS *acceptance of the afterlife in a very appropriate and utterly moving way. By the end of the monologue,* HE *is fighting back* HIS *tears as the full weight of* HIS *loss overcomes* HIM. *This monologue can be performed by a man or a woman.*

BOY: There was this tall skinny guy who got killed at the World Trade Center, along with my father. They worked in the same department, together. Currency traders. This guy had this little son—Alex—also tall and skinny. The father and Alex were really, really close. I remember my father saying that Alex and his father had started playing golf together on Staten Island, and that Alex was this really amazing golfer for his age. Alex must only be about, I dunno, eight or nine *now*. No more than that. Really cute sweet kid. After the Towers came down, my mother told me this amazing story about Alex trying to get phone calls through to Heaven, to talk to his father. He would argue with operators, supervisors, whoever would listen. He was getting really upset, so, finally, Alex comes up with this new idea, to write notes to his father, put them in balloons, and, like, float them up to Heaven. The mother doesn't have the heart to tell him the truth, so, she goes along with it, and, now, every day, Alex writes these little notes, and he and his mother take them to this party store on the corner of West Tenth Street and Greenwich Ave., and for twenty-five cents apiece, this really nice shop-guy in a turban puts Alex's notes in these balloons, which he fills with helium, and Alex and his mom take them outside and let them go, watch them fly up to Heaven. (*Beat.*) Alex is still waiting for his dad to answer him. (*Beat.*) They never found my dad's body. That makes it so totally harder for my mom to accept his death . . . that it, like, really *happened*. She goes out on our balcony, two or three times a day, and talks to him . . . to my father. She speaks slowly and clearly, like her words are gonna float up to him, like the kid's balloons. (*Beat.*) My mom's still waiting for an answer, too.

WORKING UP THE SCENE
OR MONOLOGUE

Every actor uses an individual approach when rehearsing monologues and scenes for an audition, a studio exercise, or a performance on stage. One of the most compelling and beautiful features of acting lies in those thousands of personal choices actors make in order to shape performances that are distinctly, uniquely their own. And aside from one-person shows, the actor can only enjoy this creative freedom when choosing and preparing material for auditions and studio exercises. For this reason, no single method or procedure has ever been definitively identified as the best one.

The following list of suggestions for presenting scenes and monologues serve instead as reminders of basic considerations that many actors and coaches employ. I've distilled them from dozens of interviews I've conducted, classes I've observed, workshops I've taken, and other workshops I've led over the years. I've divided them into three parts: points about staging, points about interpretation, and general points about acting etiquette. They're not hard-and-fast rules but general guidelines that can help you put to use some essentials you may have overlooked, and maybe they can even stimulate you to discover some new ideas in the material as you rehearse.

If you're a young actor who is just beginning his or her career and need this material for your auditions, acting classes, or work-shops, then these guidelines will be especially useful. And if you choose to continue to broaden your skills in this field of study, you can find many useful how-to books and DVDs on acting and auditioning.

SUGGESTIONS FOR STAGING

At an audition, introduce yourself by looking directly at the auditors, being careful to speak and move in an unforced and honest manner. As you introduce yourself and your piece, try to present a separate character that is "you": an honest, alert, and confident person who is different from the other characters in your audition pieces. Rehearse this personal introduction as carefully as you do your scenes and monologues, including your confident entrance to the stage. Look at the directors again at the end when you're finished and say, "Thank you very much." But never, ever look the auditors in the eye and try to act to them when presenting your scene or monologue. They have too much to do to serve as an enthusiastic and responsive audience.

Physicalize your acting. Your goals and changing intentions should be clearly reflected in your gestures, voice, facial expressiveness, and body language. Develop a physical characterization of gestures, postures, and movement that is every bit as rich as your psychological and vocal characterization of the role. Your physical characterization should not only reflect *who* your character is, but also *what is happening to him or her* in the scene or monologue. In short, don't present yourself as a talking head. Too many actors, drowned in a superabundance of films and television, assume that psychological conviction and belief is the only thing that matters.

Control, shape, and minimize your movements. Develop a simple pattern of blocking movements that underscores what is happening the scene or monologue. Remember that less is always more, and suppress the urge to act all over the place. Too much unnecessary movement is always distracting, just as too little is boring and non-expressive. Your body *should* and *must* respond physically to what's happening to you in the scene or monologue—there should be no short circuit between your mouth and the rest of your body. A scene or monologue that begs for movement also marks you as an amateur, lacking in confidence.

Be prepared and ready to perform. If you've properly prepared these audition pieces (e.g., for at least a year), then you should feel comfortable with them. But when you're unprepared, you're going to fidget and act up all over the place and be distracted. So rehearse well and be ready to present your stuff. Avoid stage fright from worrying about whether you'll remember your lines, whether this or that movement is the best choice to make on the line, or whether the director will notice that you're not entirely comfortable in the skin of this character. Don't wait for the day of your performance to figure those things out. And above all, take the performance seriously, like an athlete preparing for a sports event: get plenty of rest, stay fit, and be physically and mentally alert when you arrive at the studio for your presentation.

Make something happen as you speak. Be absolutely certain that the material takes you on a journey during the presentation. Remember that you must develop from the beginning, through the middle, until you come to the end of the scene or monologue where you'll stop. And at the end, you *must* be different than you were at the beginning: something *must* have changed or happened to you. Perhaps a discovery? A resolution or decision that you make? Have you fallen out of love? Have you fallen into love? What is it that your vis-à-vis has said or done to surprise you in the scene that has forced you to make new choices you didn't anticipate? Identify the places in the scene or monologue where all these events occur, and attack each new stage of this development clearly and strongly so we can see what's happening to you. Make something happen in the scene or monologue. "Event your scene," as the great acting teacher Michael Shurtleff was fond of repeating, and *play those events*.

Establish eye contact with your vis-à-vis whenever possible. In monologues, locate your vis-à-vis in only one place to avoid confusing your listeners—preferably in the audience. Stage your scene or monologue by playing to the house as much as possible in order to open the scene out. In two-character scene presentations, remain upstage of your acting partner as much as possible because it is your audition, not your partner's, and you wish to be seen more. Of course, you must involve him or her in the scene— energy in the playing must be shared and the chemistry of the relationship must be palpable for the scene to work properly. But stage the scene so that you receive the primary visual focus most of the time.

Never pantomime a prop such as a telephone, a doorknob, a weapon, and the like. You can "bring a friend" with you onstage (a matchbox, a coin, a pair of spectacles) in order to ground yourself and have something concrete to touch or use in the scene. But lose the bogus telephone, and never speak to a vis-à-vis in an empty chair. Auditions are phony enough as it is. Try instead to connect with something or someone real. Even hearing an imaginative sound with belief is more real than lamely pantomiming a knock on a nonexistent door while stamping your feet.

In an audition, always arrange and re-arrange the furniture— usually a chair and/or a table—before beginning. This helps you relax and take more control of the performance space, and also provides a useful break between your pieces when presenting more than one. This simple action will loosen up your physical movement and express confidence and control to the auditors watching you— which they will be doing from the moment you first appear, long before you open your mouth to speak.

Never stare at the stage floor. There is nothing there; create a relationship with someone.

Consider carefully whether you should actually sit in a chair. Most actors find that sitting robs them of energy during the performance. Consider what other ways you might use that chair or prop: to lean against, to move or adjust slightly, and so on. On the other hand, rising from the chair or sitting down on it once during your monologue or scene can be an effective physical action that marks a beat change in your character's development.

Get yourself a director. The more talented the better, of course. But anyone can simply watch your audition and tell you whether they can hear you, or whether the monologue or scene seemed clear, or whether it touched them emotionally. Have them close their eyes and *listen* to your speech pattern in order to see where you're slurring your words, rushing too hastily, or dragging the pace. Have them cover their ears and *watch* your performance in order to note all the nonverbal cues that you're sending: flicking your loose hair, licking your lips, flapping your hands, or remaining physically limp or woodenly tense during the performance. You *need* this "outside eye" to note these things because most of us lack the necessary objectivity to identify these characteristics in ourselves, even when we watch ourselves on camera or hear our recorded voices.

TIPS ON INTERPRETATION

Every scene you will ever do will always be based on relationships. This is the single most important piece of advice I took from my workshops with Michael Shurtleff, and I've found that it works in theater, film, commercials, and many other settings. It holds true in the acting studio, in performances, and in auditions. Build that relationship by reading the entire play and by filling in the blanks between you and your vis-à-vis with your improvised backstory, biography, and the moment before. Make some *chemistry* happen in performance with your real or imaginary vis-à-vis because that's what we come to the theater to see. We're all emotional vampires in the theater, seeking *drama* in our boring lives.

You will die if you cannot win over your vis-à-vis here and now. Build urgency into your scenes and monologues because plays are not written about the ordinary moments in life, about everyday relationships. Only this vis-à-vis *here* and *now* can scratch your itch by giving you what you desperately need. This becomes especially challenging with monologues that must have a clear vis-à-vis whom you're fighting to win over. Eliminate reminiscence, nostalgia, and poetic lyricism from your monologues, and instead score an impact on your vis-à-vis with your words.

Make bold choices in the scene or monologue for clearly playing the pattern of beats. The great acting teacher Uta Hagen regarded this as the single most effective technique in the actor's toolbox: clearly playing the pattern of beats that you establish in the scene. As I mentioned earlier about physicalizing those beat changes in your monologue or scene, be certain that you're also portraying that overall development from beginning to end in your voice and in your body energy. Something definitely *happens* to you in a good monologue or scene. If the material doesn't contain those changes, then either choose material that does or invent and improvise your character's changes and alternative choices on your own.

Be ready to make changes. Auditors will frequently ask you to try a different characterization or read the part in a different way in order to see whether you can take direction. ("Read it instead like you hate each other." "Read it like it was the saddest story you've ever experienced." "Read it like you're totally baffled and challenged by the ideas.") Some directors may want to see whether you can make your acting choices more specific than you did in the general reading. You don't want to be classified as a one-note performer who can't take direction.

TIPS ON AUDITION ETIQUETTE

Come prepared for your audition. Auditors are evaluating you from the moment you enter the room. If memorized material is required, be sure that it's solidly memorized. (Once again, live with your audition material for at least a year before presenting it.) Stay alert, keep yourself fit, and be ready with plenty of energy and focus for the day of the audition. Remember that these people are casting now—not two weeks from now when you might feel better from your cold, or later this morning after a few shots of coffee. Nothing marks an amateur more than lack of preparedness, and there are too many disciplined, hard-working actors waiting in the hallway who are hungry for roles. Directors don't want to waste time on lazy people when it comes to casting.

Dress appropriately for the audition. Those people conducting the auditions enjoy interacting with others who appear confident and successful, and who also have some self-respect, because they take care of their personal appearance. Remember that your clothes are costumes that are always making a statement about you. Avoid over-dressing in a formal way, just as you should avoid dressing like a careless slob in a professional situation. There are three rules for clothing at an audition: 1) you should feel comfortable in your clothes; 2) you should be able to physically move and express in your clothes; and 3) you should wear *something* that helps the auditors to remember you—a colorful sash or scarf, or a colorful jacket you can simply put on or remove for another look. And above all, no sexy bare midriffs or muscle shirts; people can buy skin on the street without going to the trouble of attracting it to an audition. Casting is serious business.

Make a point of knowing each and every person in the room. This is an added opportunity to audition yourself to casting people outside of the audition proper. It builds the personal impression that you wish to score as an enhancement of your acting. The key person to identify is, of course, the director or casting director(s). But you never know who may be watching, because theater is a small world, and you may be called back months later for another role in different project just because someone remembered a good performance you gave. And be sure to ask questions—particularly of the director—if you have the time.

In two-character scene auditions, place your acting partner downstage. This will help you stay open to the auditors and avoid upstaging yourself when speaking to your vis-à-vis. Many acting partners don't understand this because they think the scene is also about them. In an audition, the scene is about you. Only in acting class should you make an exception to this rule, because in a class setting, the scene will seem unbalanced when only one of the characters receives major emphasis.

In an audition, never speak directly to the auditors. They are not your vis-à-vis; they are your critics and judges. Let them do their judgmental thing without forcing them to respond emotionally to whatever you're doing onstage. Proper casting requires a lot of objectivity on the part of the directors or auditors. Locate your vis-à-vis in the house somewhere—perhaps slightly over the heads of the auditors, or just off the apron of the stage left or right—and keep the person there. Don't have the vis-à-vis move around during your scene or monologue, because this just seems confusing and unfocused to listeners.

Never apologize for mistakes or request to start over. Keep going no matter what, even if you have to invent half of what follows. Re-starts never produce better acting; they only embarrass the directors, who have to witness your embarrassment and discomfort due to your unpreparedness. Apologies only express your inability to overcome your nervousness and lack of confidence. Mumbling some self-criticism after a performance or an audition can only destroy the good impressions you have just created.

When asked to "please do it again" with a few changes, never change your original performance completely. Yes, the director may wish to see how you take direction and how much additional talent you may have when he or she asks you to "do it a little differently." But a director will never ask you for this if your initial performance was terrible—there must have been some good things there for the director to want to spend additional time observing you. So, don't discard the choices you made in your original performance when asked to do it again; build upon those choices and add just what the director asks you to do on the second attempt.

Wacko is not original or creative, and neither is vulgarity. Remember that there is nothing you can show or say to the directors that will surprise or shock them. They've all been around the block. Unpredictability and originality should emerge from your acting choices, not from your personal manner. Time is critical in the entertainment business—particularly in media work. You don't want to force the auditors to wonder if they're going to have to handhold your emotions through each and every rehearsal. They *will not* keep you supplied with meds in order to get the job done. There are just too many dependable and creative actors out there to hire instead of you.

Never leave the audition until you've been dismissed. Many directors will ask actors to remain for improvs after delivering their prepared audition, or to receive information about callbacks. Perhaps a director will want to ask you a couple of questions (remember that casting is only 50 percent talent—the rest depends on whether you have a friendly personality that others can live and work with for four to six weeks of rehearsal and performances). Most of the time the directors will simply say "Thank you" following your performance, which is your cue to exit the stage or the room. Don't dally by asking when you'll be notified, or if they liked it, or anything else. Be businesslike and make a professional exit by letting everyone believe that you have another audition waiting down the street.

PLAY SOURCES AND ACKNOWLEDGMENTS

Other Monologue Books